EXMOOR AND BEYOND

THE PHOTOGRAPHY OF

MICHAEL MILTON

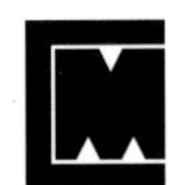

CREATIVE MONOCHROME
CONTEMPORARY PORTFOLIO SERIES

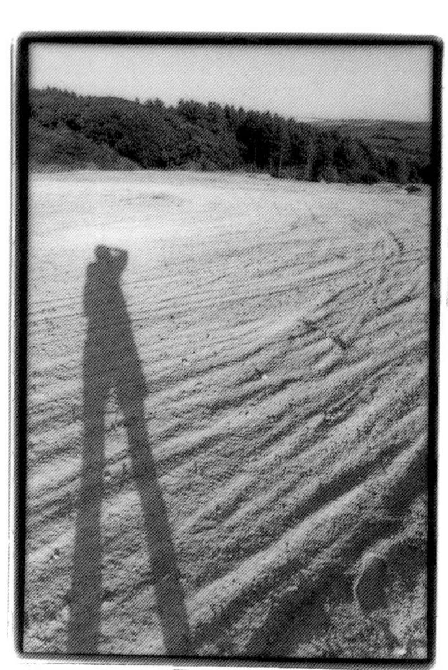

MICHAEL MILTON's interest in photography started with the desire to record his extensive travels in Europe and Australia. He subsequently studied photography in South Wales and was employed by De Vere Photographic prior to working as a freelance photographer in London. He was a silver medallist in the 1996 Best of Friends Awards. Currently working from his home county of Devon, his interests in photography include portraiture and figure work as well as landscape. Michael's work is represented by The Special Photographers Company, London.

ACKNOWLEDGEMENT

Special thanks to Don Nickolls for his help and encouragement with this project.

EXMOOR AND BEYOND

The photography of
MICHAEL MILTON

Published in the UK by Creative Monochrome Ltd,
20 St Peters Road, Croydon, Surrey, CR0 1HD.

British Library Cataloguing-in-Publication Data:
A catalogue record for this book is available from the British Library.

ISBN 1 873319 24 X
First edition, 1996

Printed in England by Penshurst Press, Buckingham House,
Longfield Road, Tunbridge Wells, Kent, TN2 3EY

Introduction

Michael Milton

Walking towards Dunkery Beacon again. This time it is December and an icy wind blows into my face. Arriving at the top, I have a 360° view: to the north, across the Bristol Channel to the black hills of Wales; to the east, the Quantocks; to the south, the tors of Dartmoor, and to the west, the hills of Exmoor and North Devon. The light is flat today, so there will be no pictures, but I am alive with the familiar thrill of being at the highest point on Exmoor.

I was born in North Devon and grew up here. It has exerted a magnetic attraction on me ever since. Even while working in London as a commercial photographer in the 1980s, the weekends would often see me returning 'home'. Walks on Exmoor were a pleasant way to relax on a Sunday. At first, I left the tools of my trade in the city, but gradually my increasing appreciation of the nature of the light and the textures of the landscape set my photography along a new path. Somehow my exile had brought me not only to a greater appreciation of this familiar landscape, but to a fuller understanding of my place within it.

There is a wonderful tradition of landscape photography in this country, but I wanted to look deeper into the structure of a scene, to examine the interaction of the elements and the earth: rocks piercing the soil, weathered, shattered and crumbling into stones and gravel; caked soil breaking into clods; clay sleek after the rain, and twigs and grass woven into mats. The multiplicity of textures interact in different ways, sometimes jarring and jostling, at other times forming a mystical harmony.

Taking a more distant view, patterns in rock and bark blur to be echoed fractal-like in the greater landscape: the rough open moorland runs up against the beech hedges of angular upland farms; dull leaden clouds wrap sheets of winter rain around mottled downs; chaotic gushing streams cut the floors of valleys, smoothed and rounded by Ice Age glaciers; densely forested combes shelter from the wind, and woods edge onto splintered crags that pitch hundreds of feet into the sea.

To the west, the cliffs of Exmoor climb down into a gentler landscape, the coastline turns south away from the Bristol Channel to face full into the oncoming Atlantic. The secluded bays and long beaches of the Taw and Torridge estuary absorb and dissipate the massive energy of the ocean's surf.

Further south, across Bideford Bay is the parish of Hartland. I always find a visit to Hartland Point a humbling and amazing experience. There is an ancient and remote feel to the headland that the Romans called 'the promontory of Hercules'. It keeps calling me back to explore new perspectives and lighting conditions.

The sedimentary action of old rivers and seas, the folds and fractures in the earth's crust, infernal heat and pressure: all have combined to provide rich raw materials for the elements to set to work on here. Ferocious gales, biting frost, wind, rain and sun carve bizarre abstract forms and shapes reminiscent of strange mythical and primeval beasts.

Waves gnaw betwen the layers of soft shale and hard metamorphic rock to form bore holes and caverns. Energy from the wind draws flexing sinews into the faces of the waves, whose endless breakers sort sand and pebbles by weight into stratifications along the beach. Hollows in the rock allow salt water, abandoned by retreating tides, to settle into calm pools, and beneath their shimmering surfaces, primitive creatures find shelter.

All this pattern and order is created by the unthinking hand of the elements – a hand that will remain at work even if we go the way of the dinosaurs. This series of images is my homage to these natural forces. The photographs attempt to depict the essence of the landscape of Exmoor and North Devon rather than to present a comprehensive travel guide. I hope my love for this landscape and my awe of the elemental forces which have fashioned it will shine through these photographs and capture the heart and soul of Exmoor and beyond.

PORTFOLIO

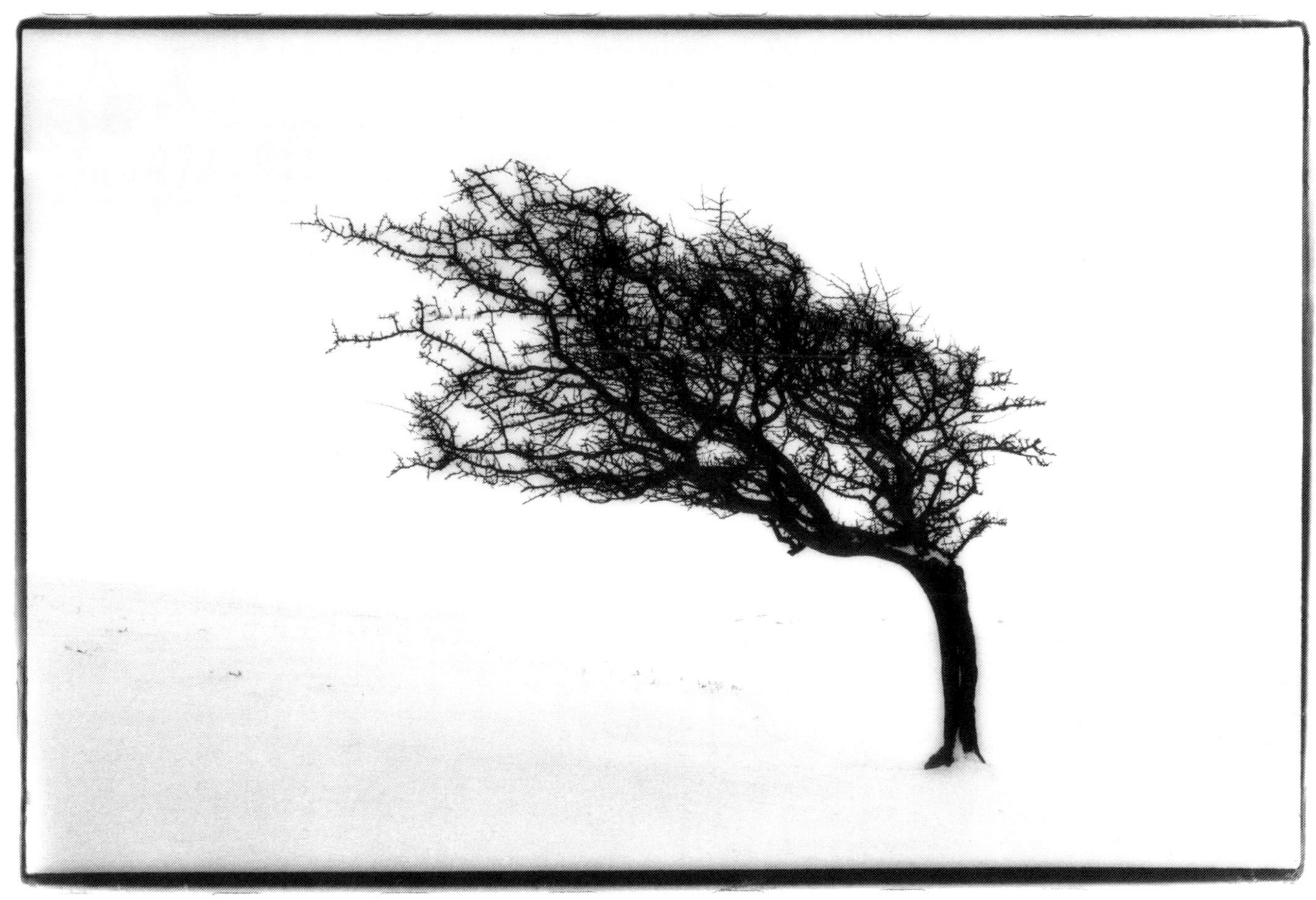

1
Shillstone Hill
Brendon Common, Exmoor

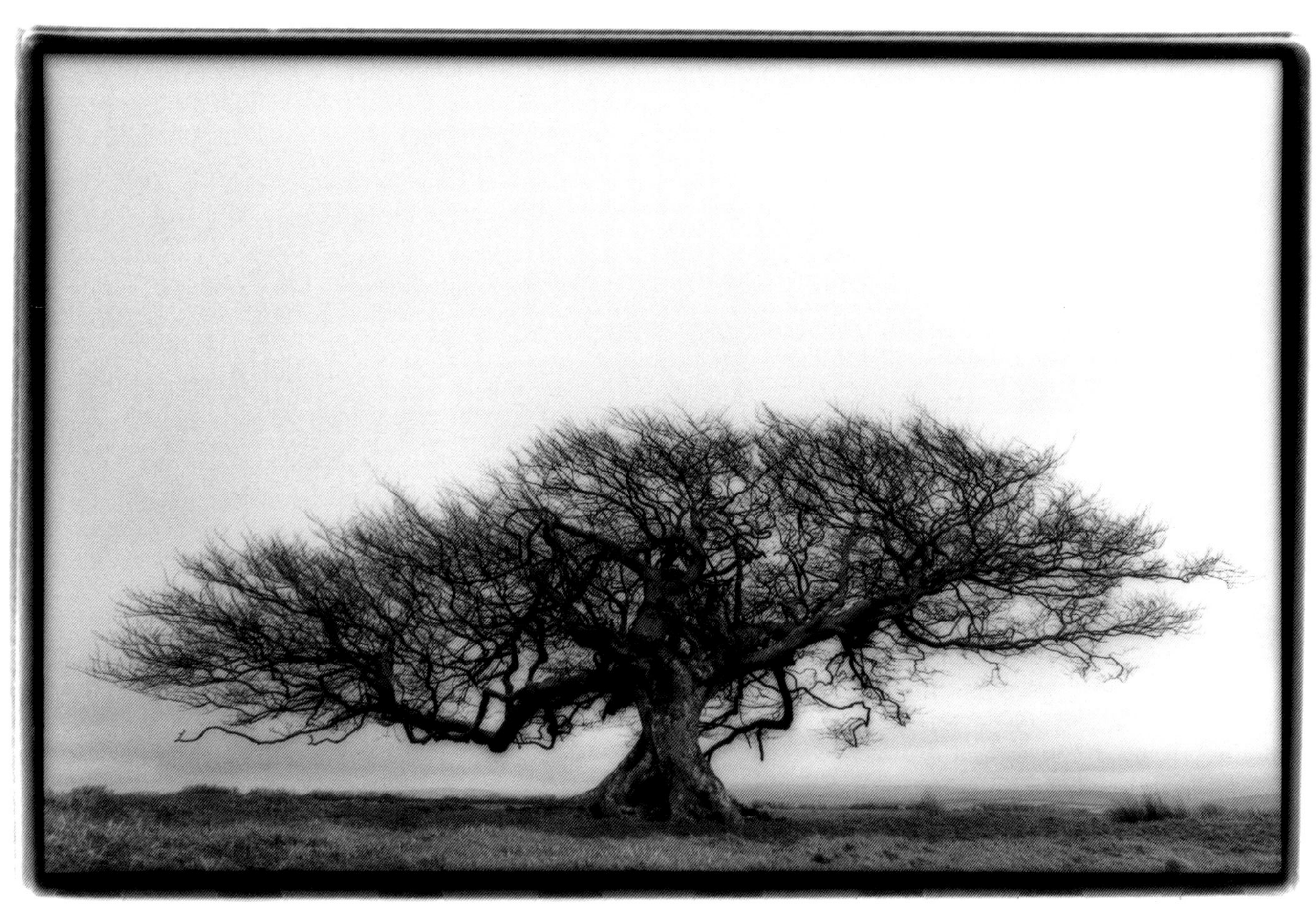

2

Lone tree I

Near Dunkery, Exmoor

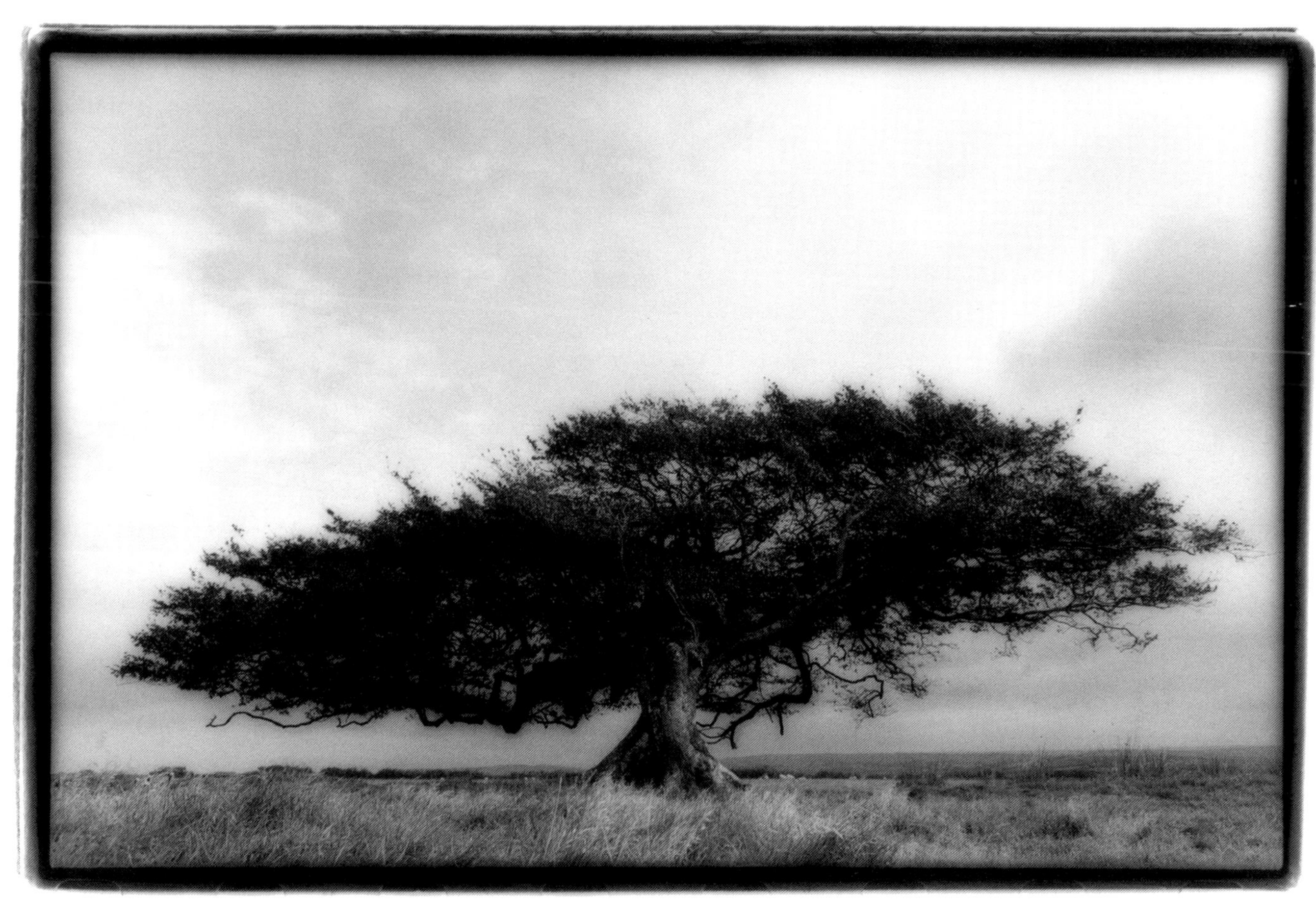

3

Lone tree II

Near Dunkery, Exmoor

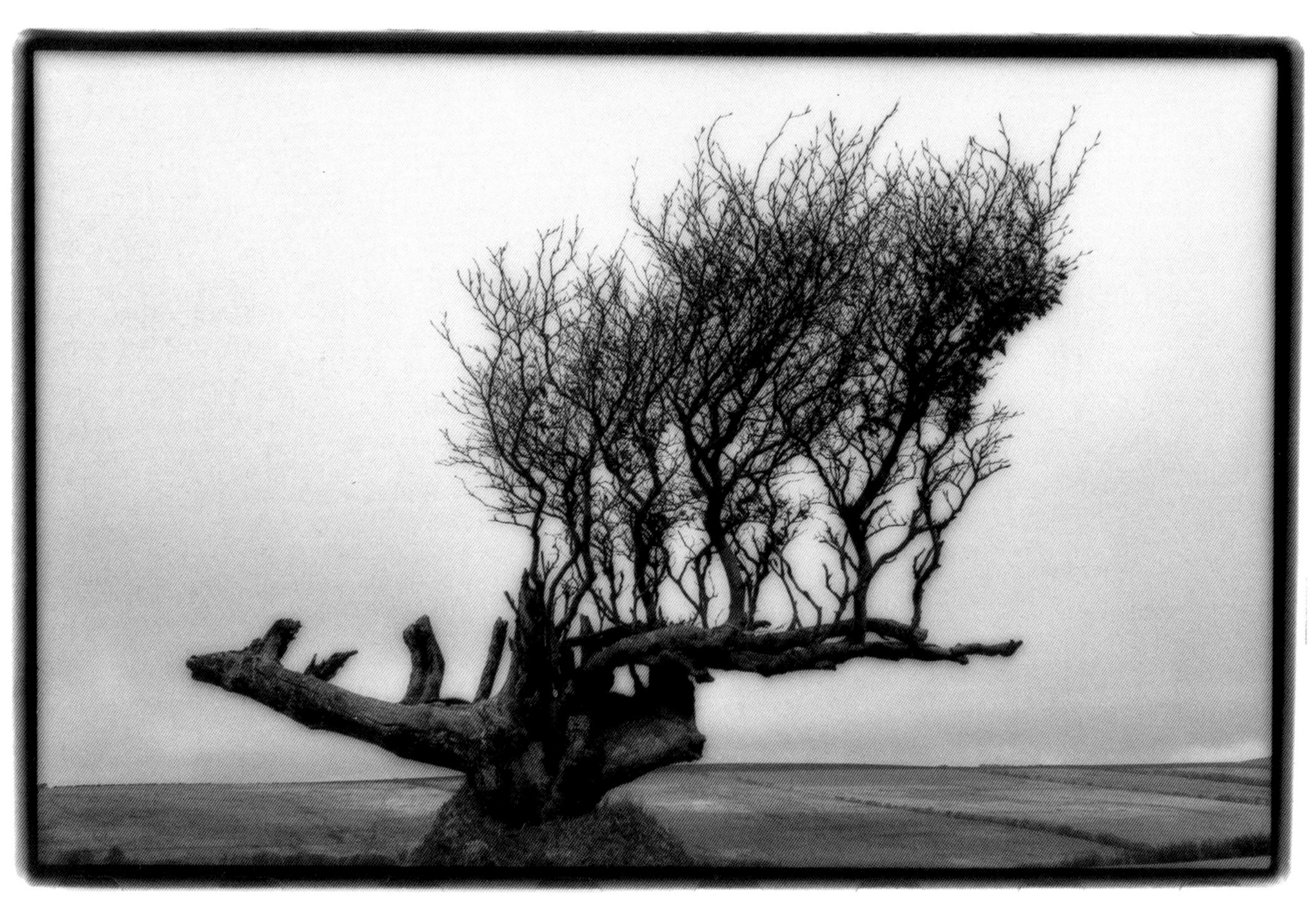

4
Laid beech remnant
Prescott Down, Exmoor

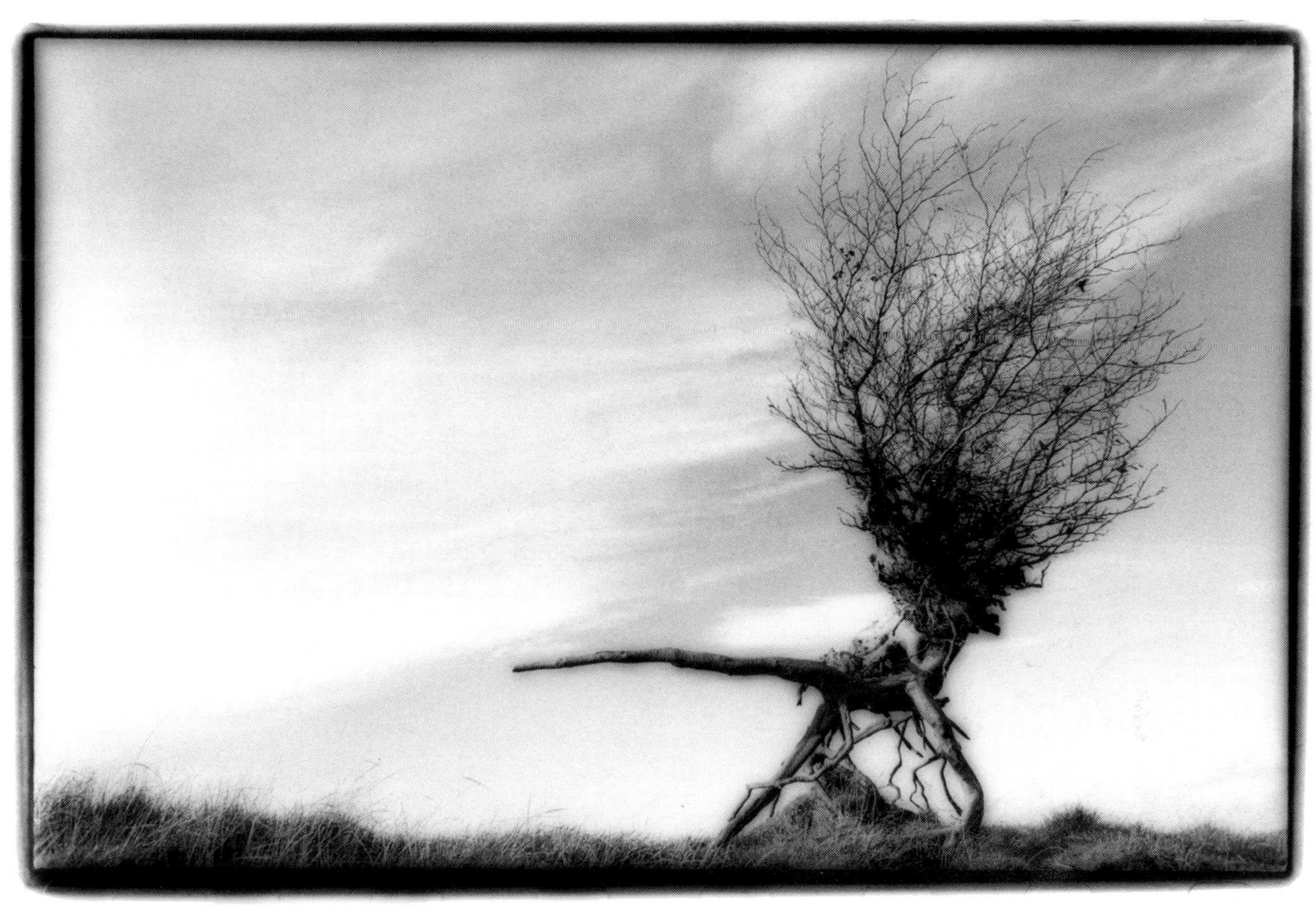

5
High farmland
Above Cheriton, Exmoor

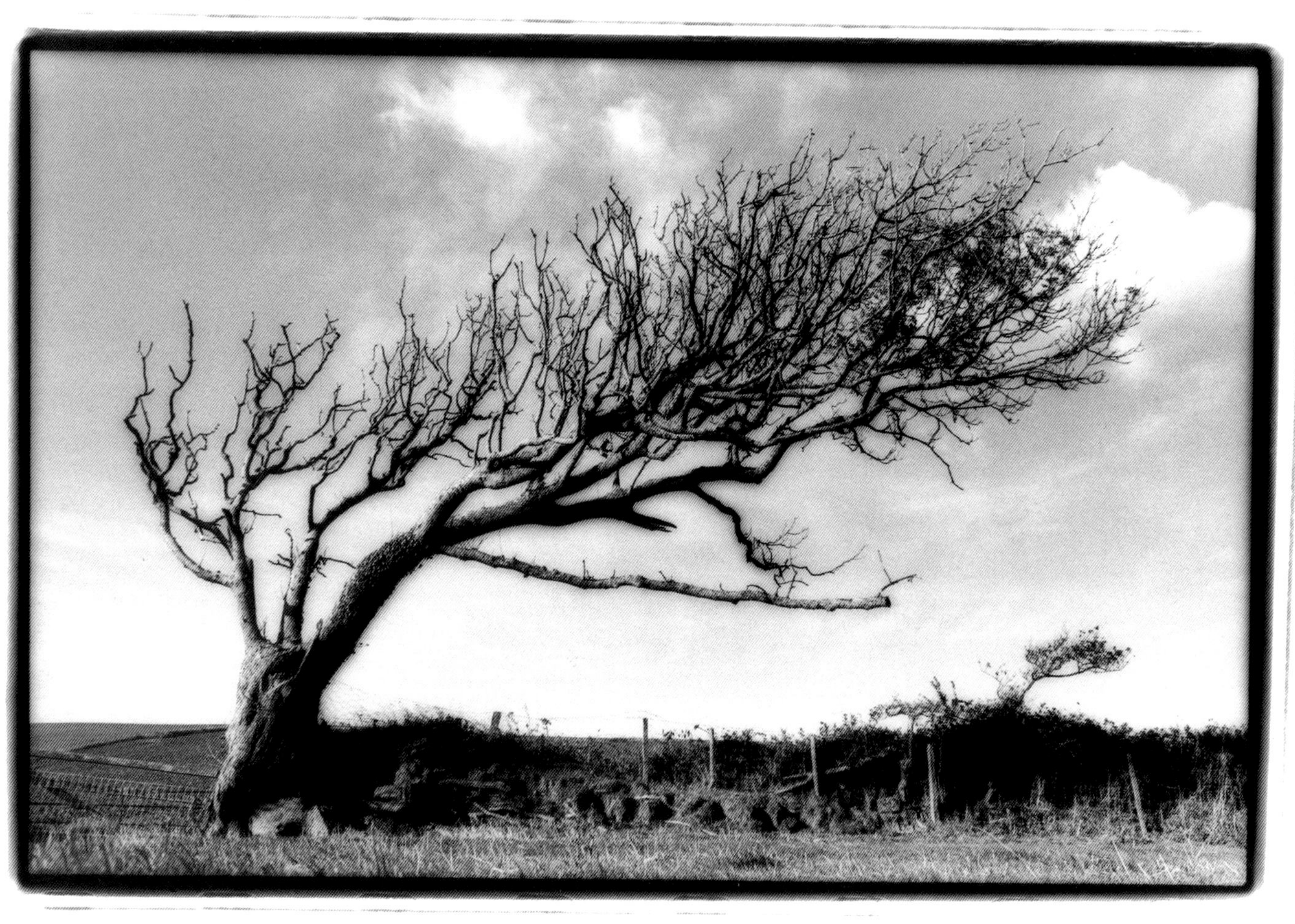

6
Weather-beaten tree
Near Braunton

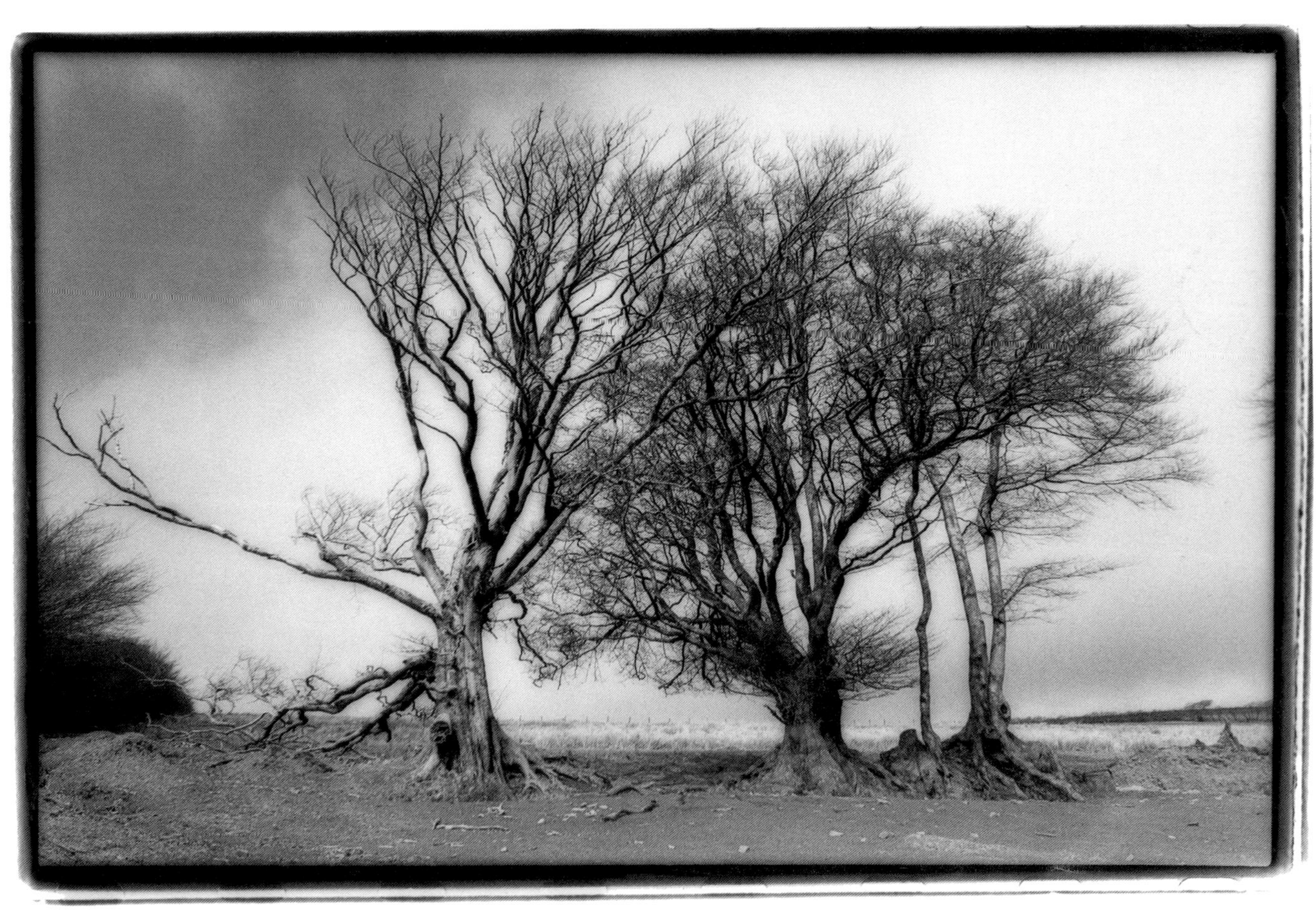

7
Beech trees
Sharcott, Exmoor

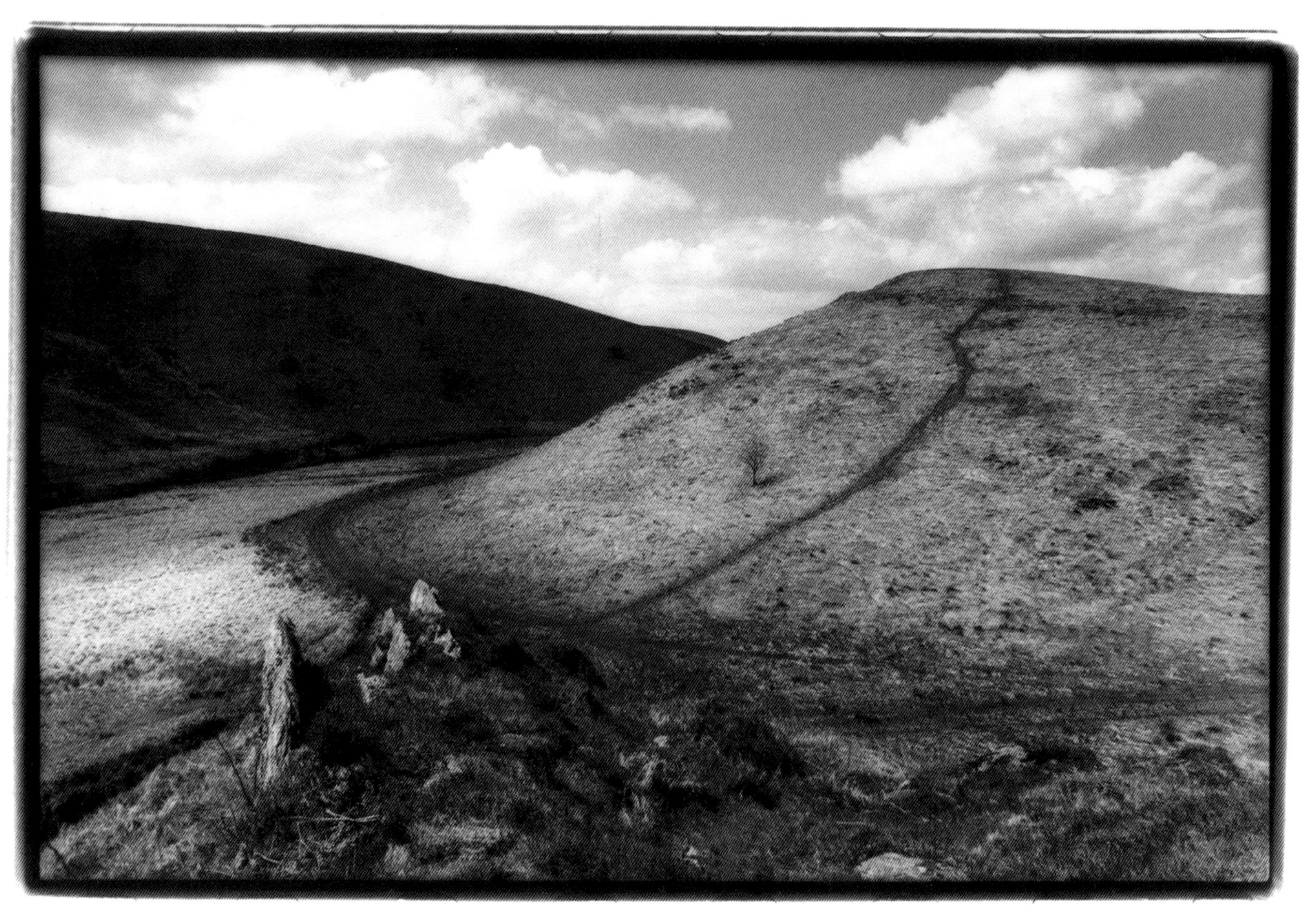

8
Cow Castle
Exmoor

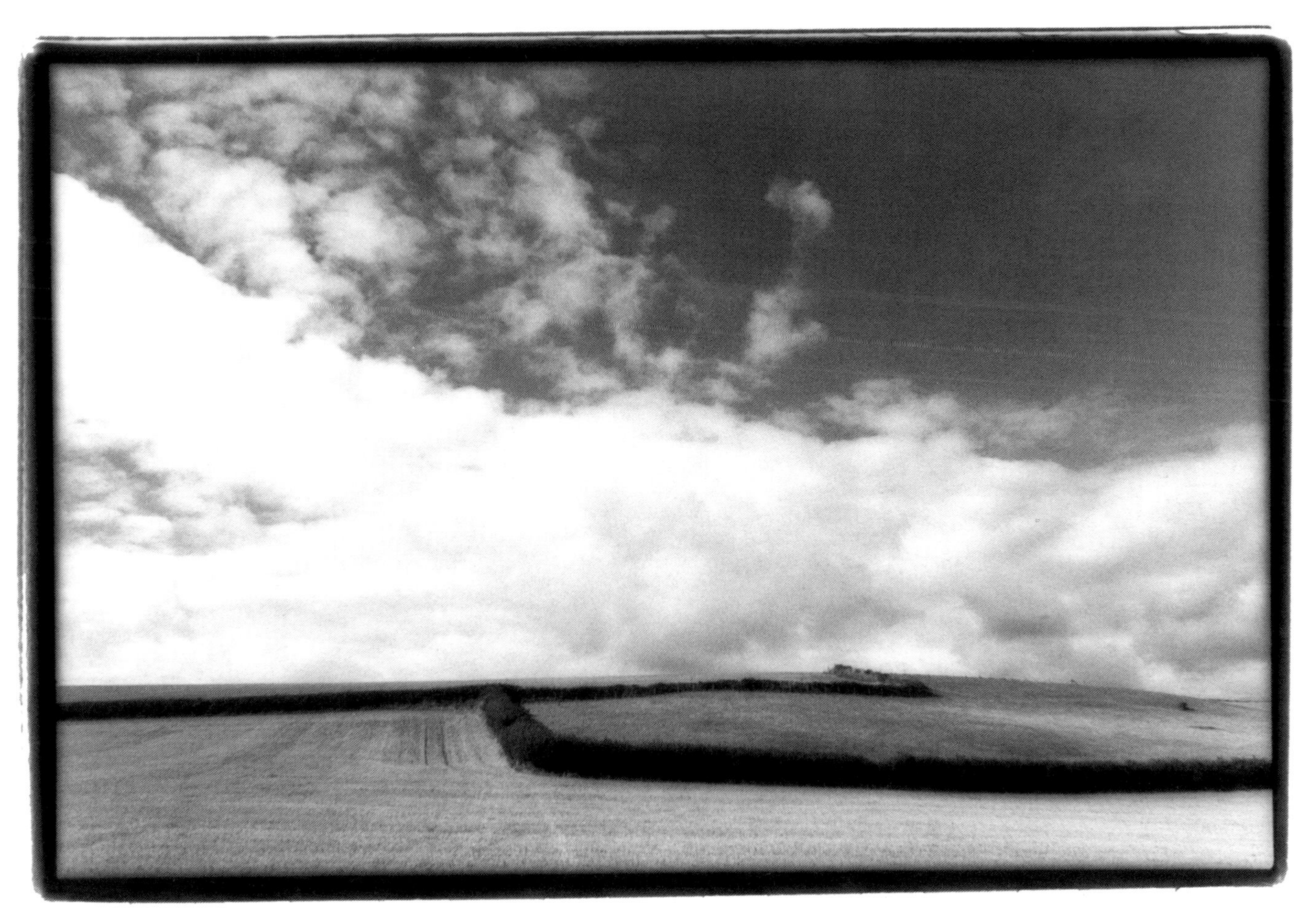

9
'No Mans Land'
Near Georgeham

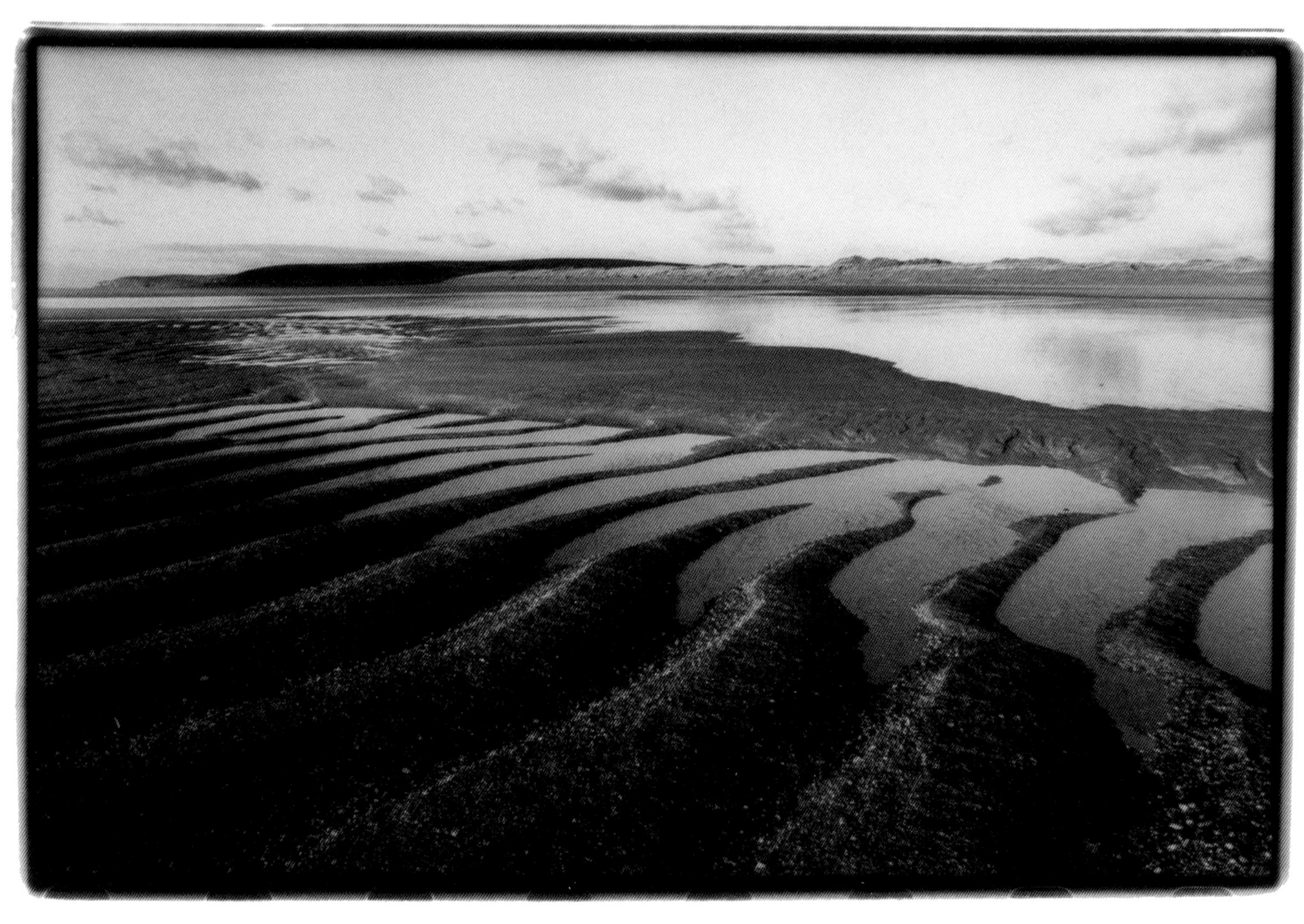

10
North Tail
Crow Point

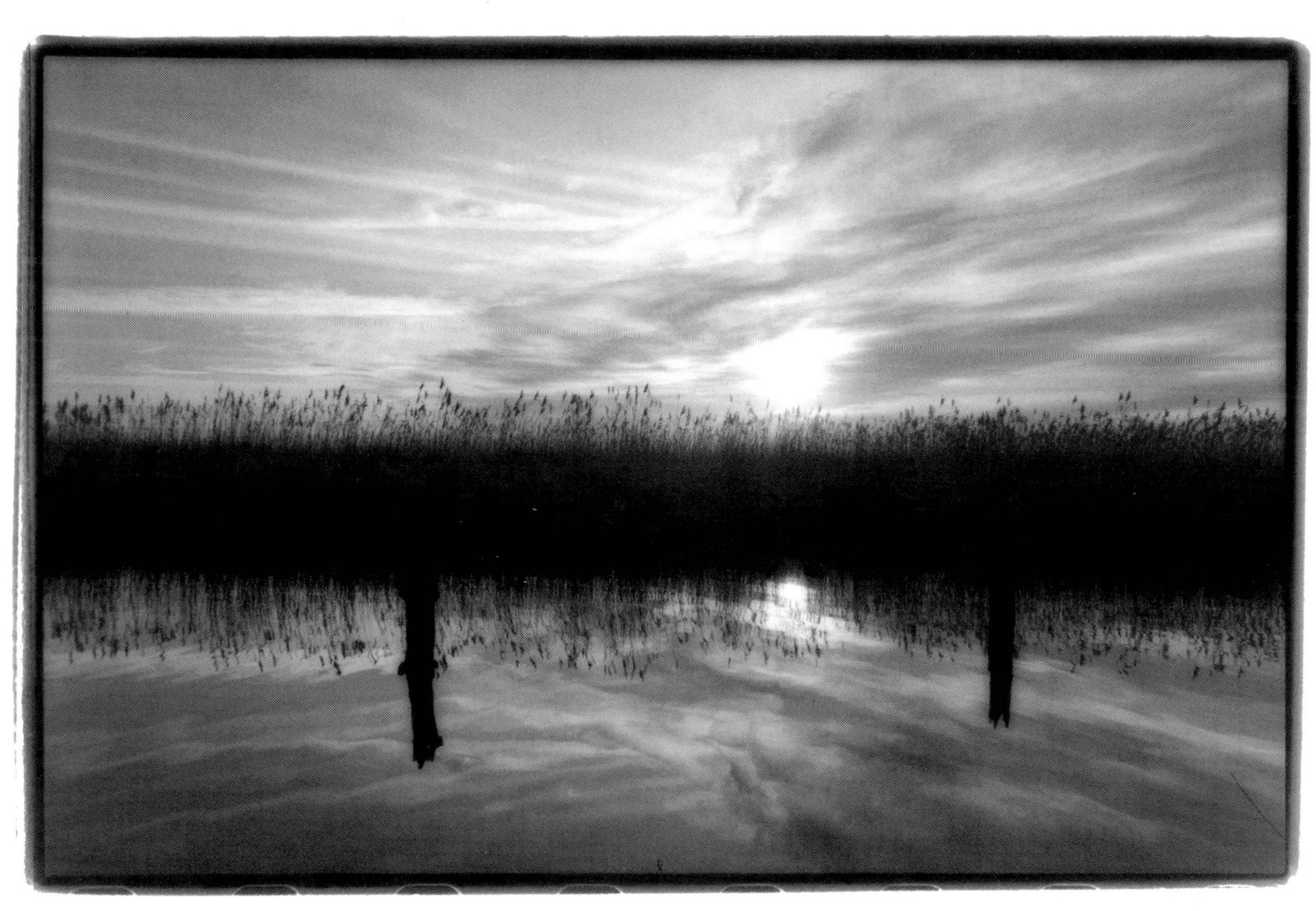

11
Reed beds
Braunton

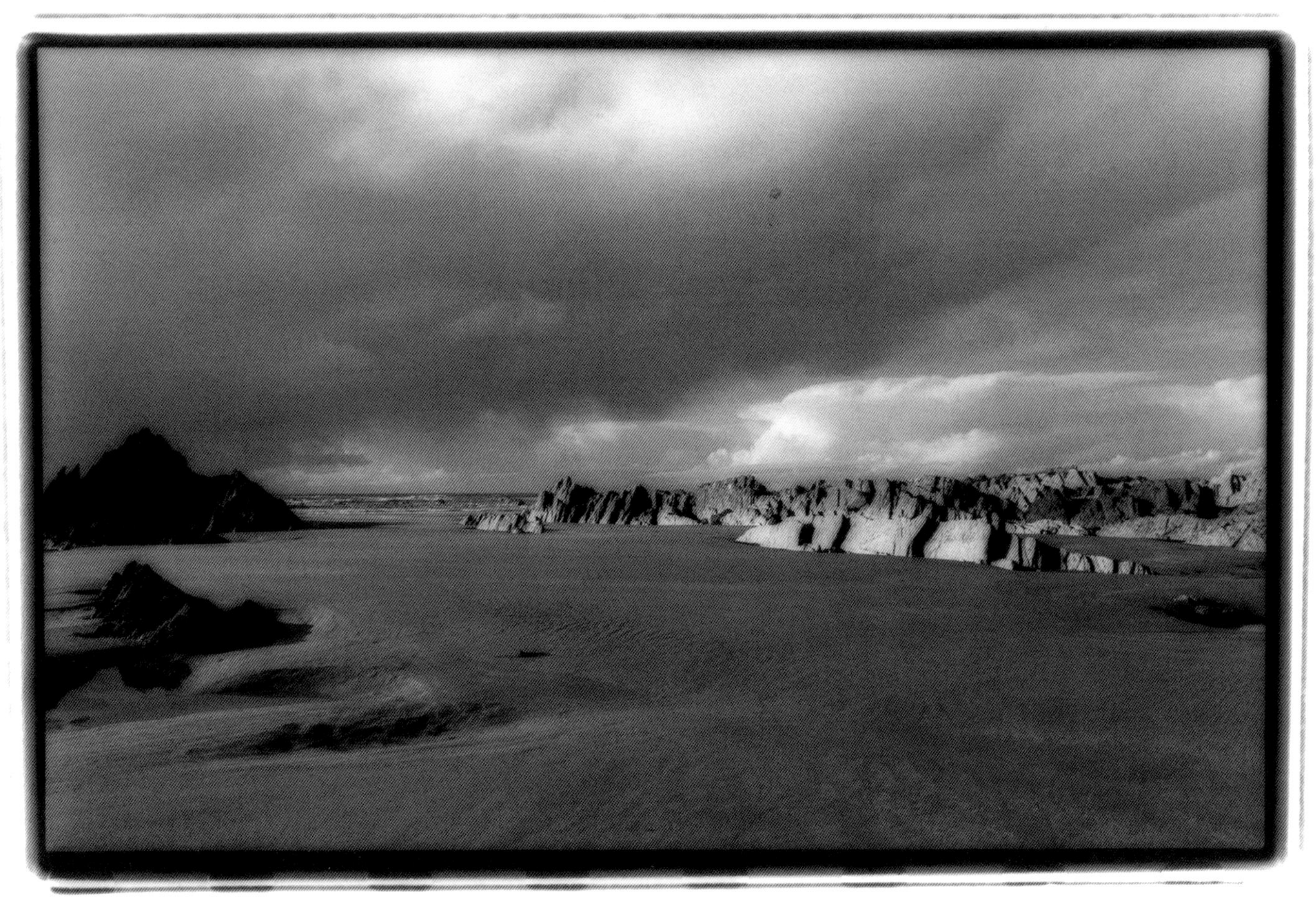

12
Rockham Bay
Mort-Ho

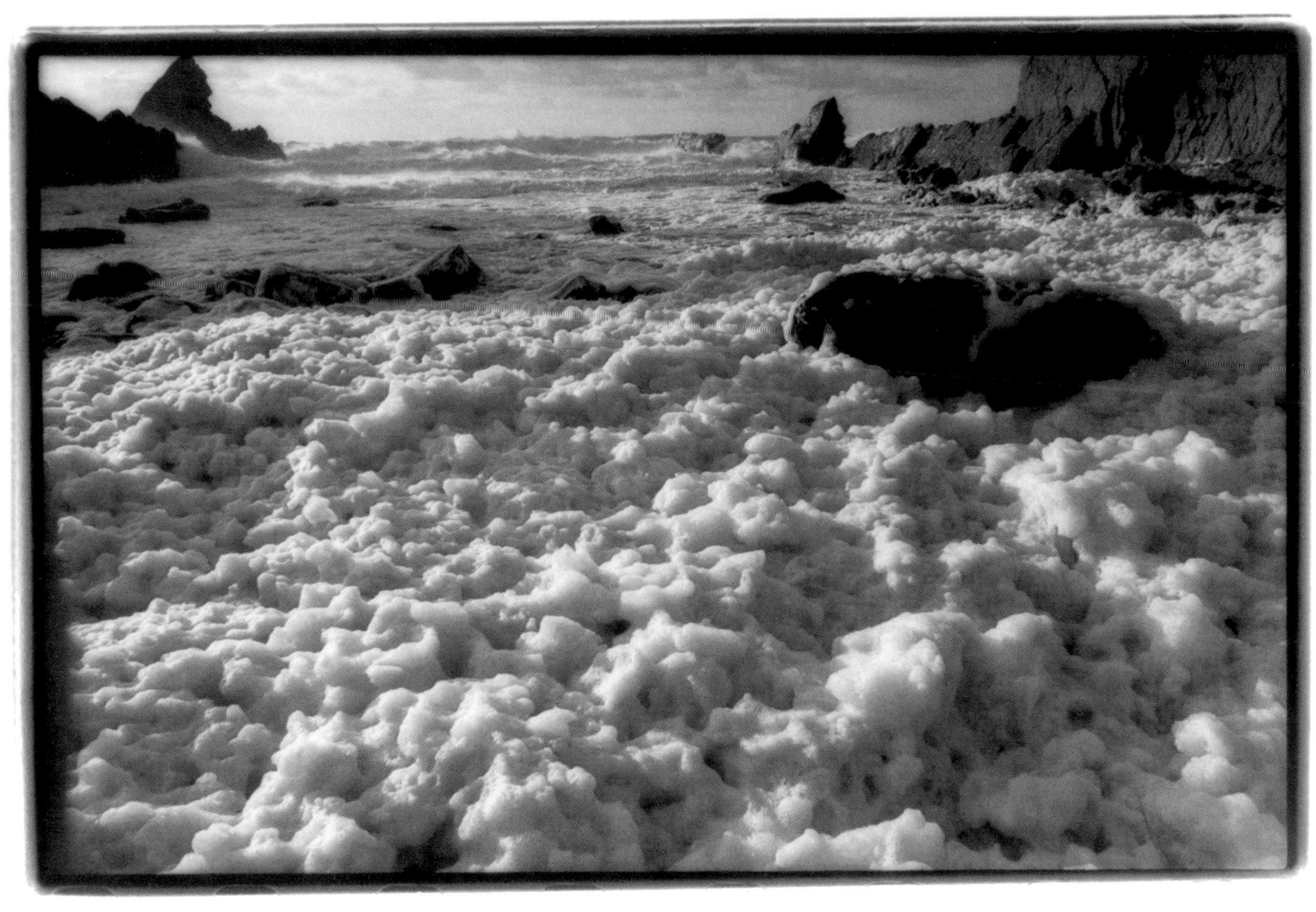

13
Bloom algae
Dyer Lookout, Hartland

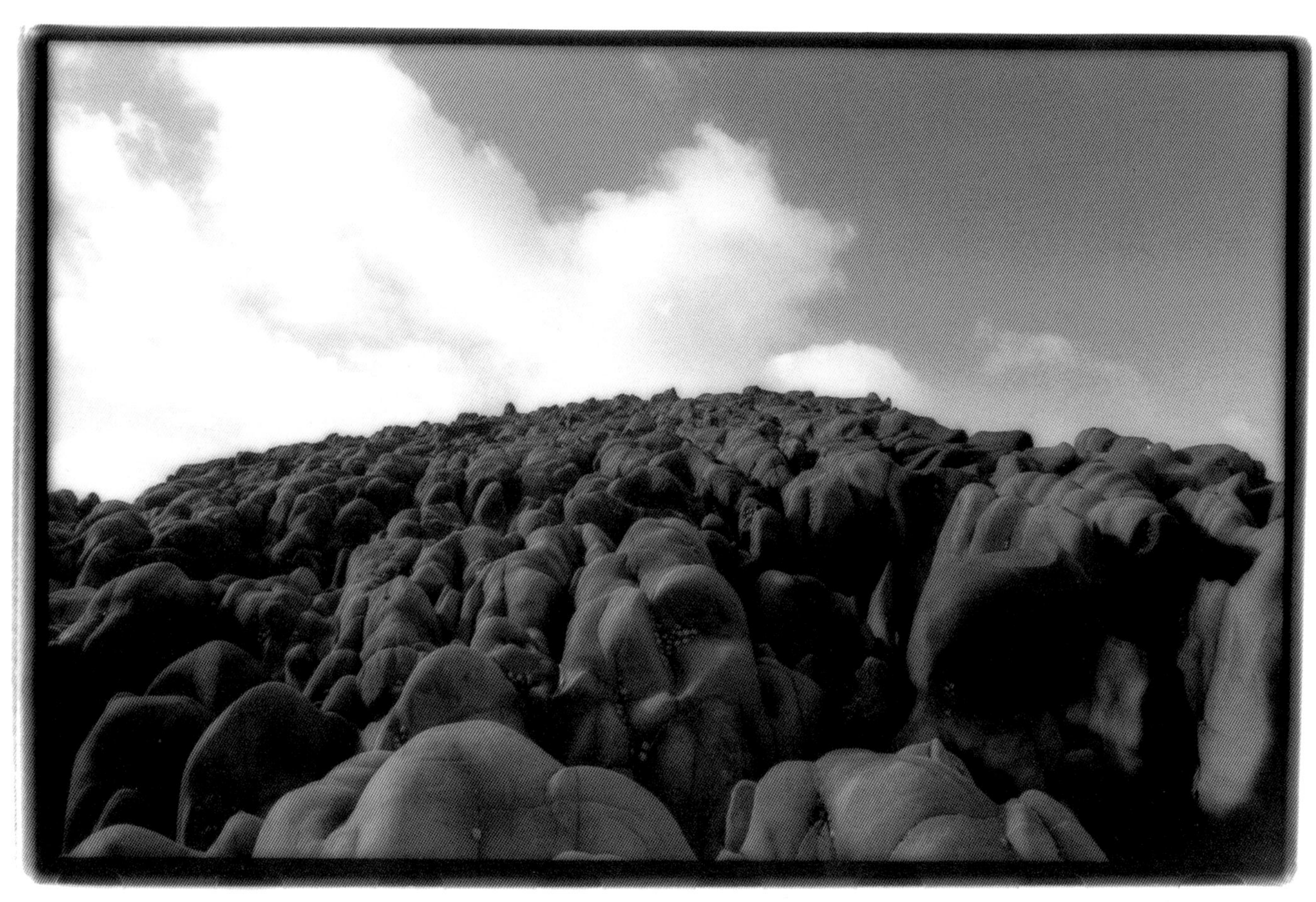

14

Pepper boulder carpet

Damehole Point, Hartland

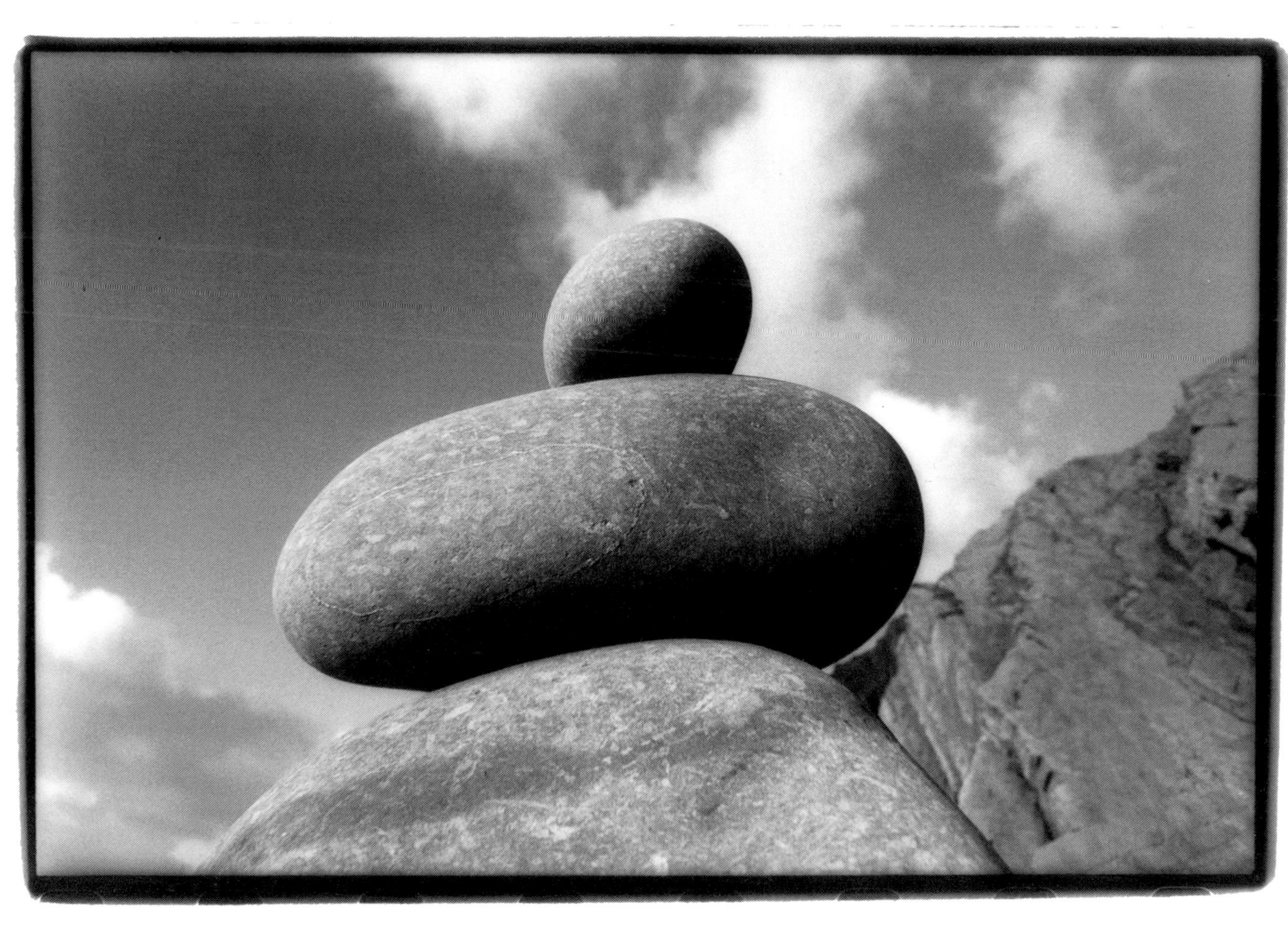

15
Nature's sculpture
Near Hartland Quay

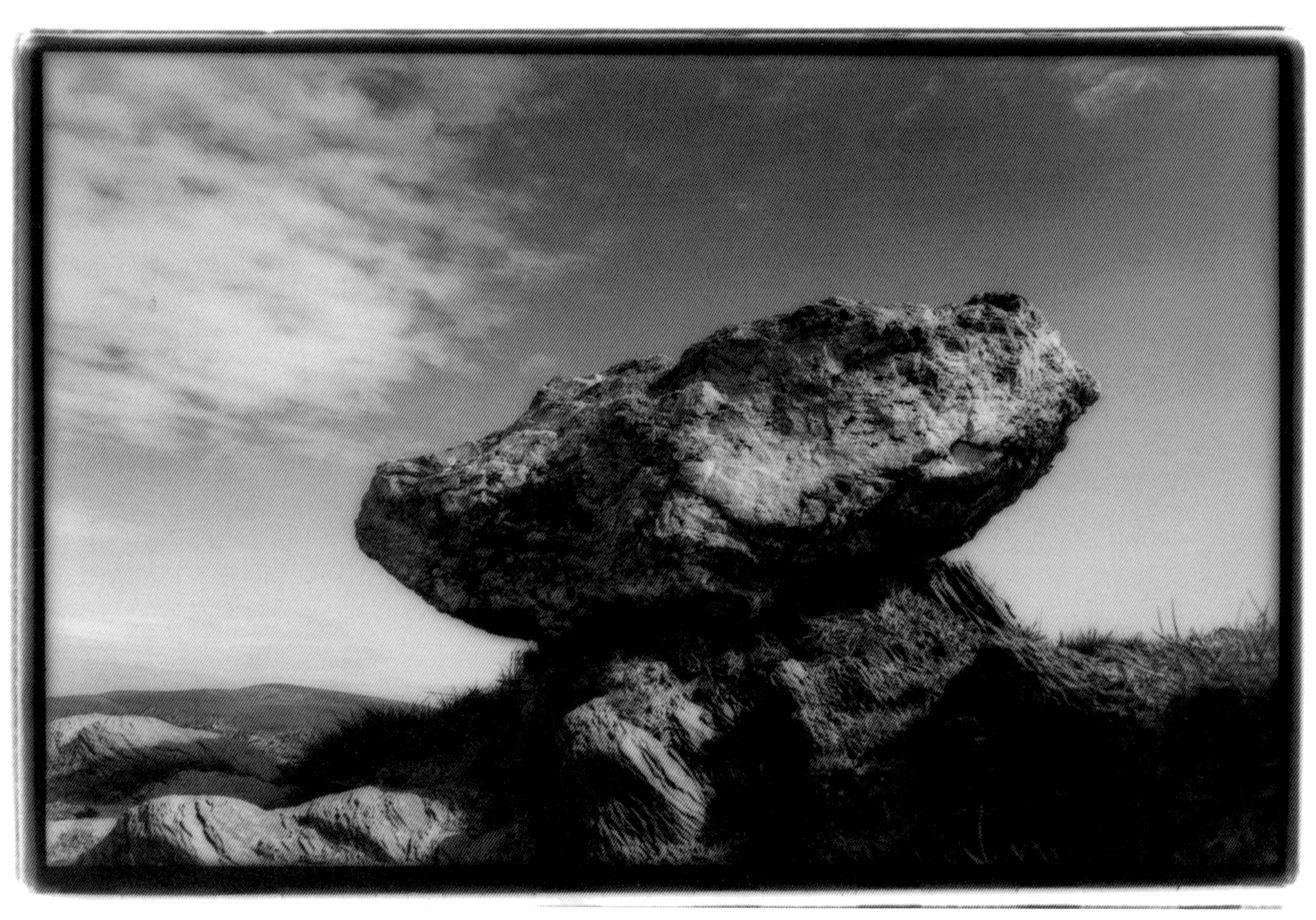

16
Quartz boulder on natural plinth
Bodstone Barton, Exmoor

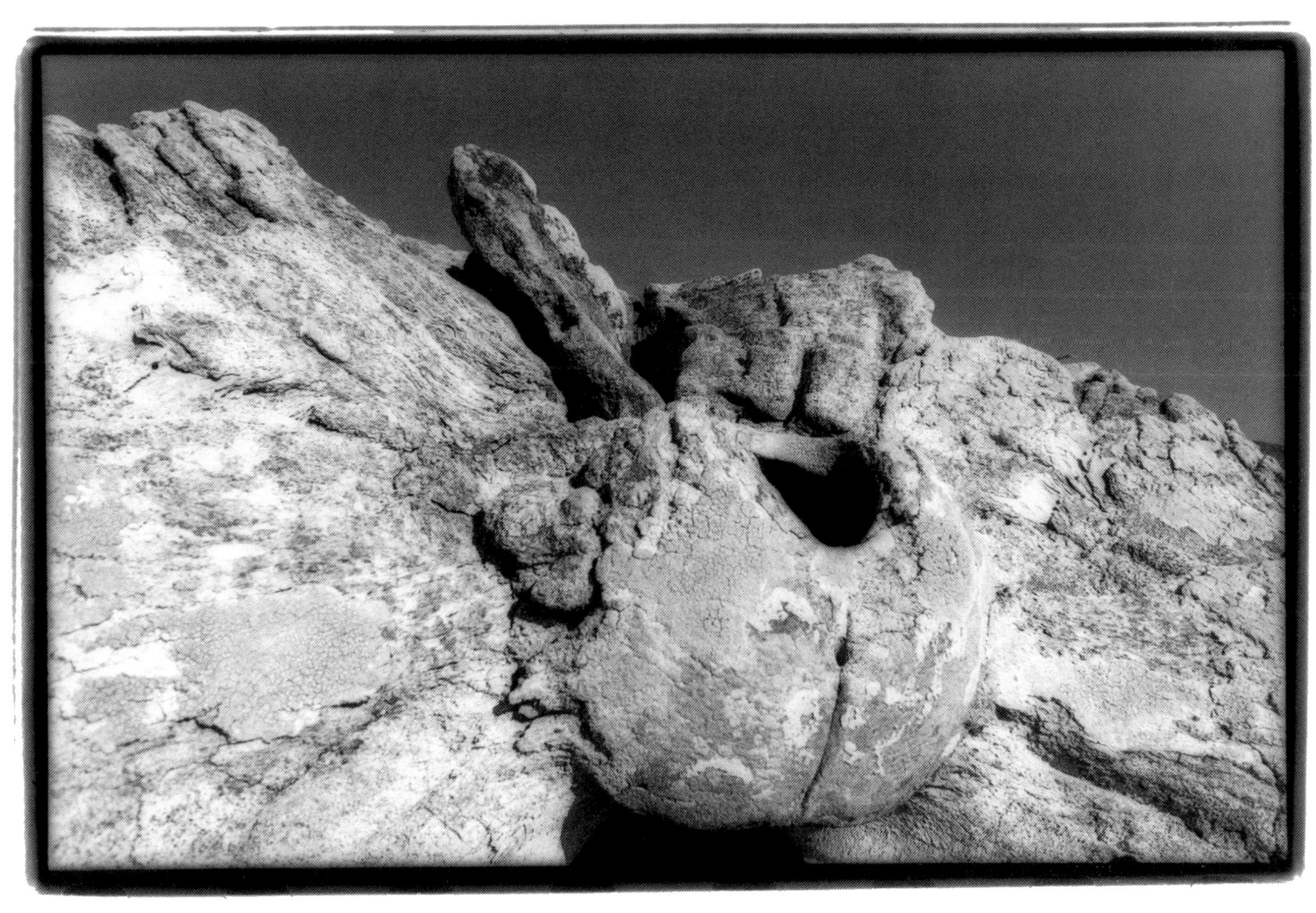

17
Wale Skull
Croyde

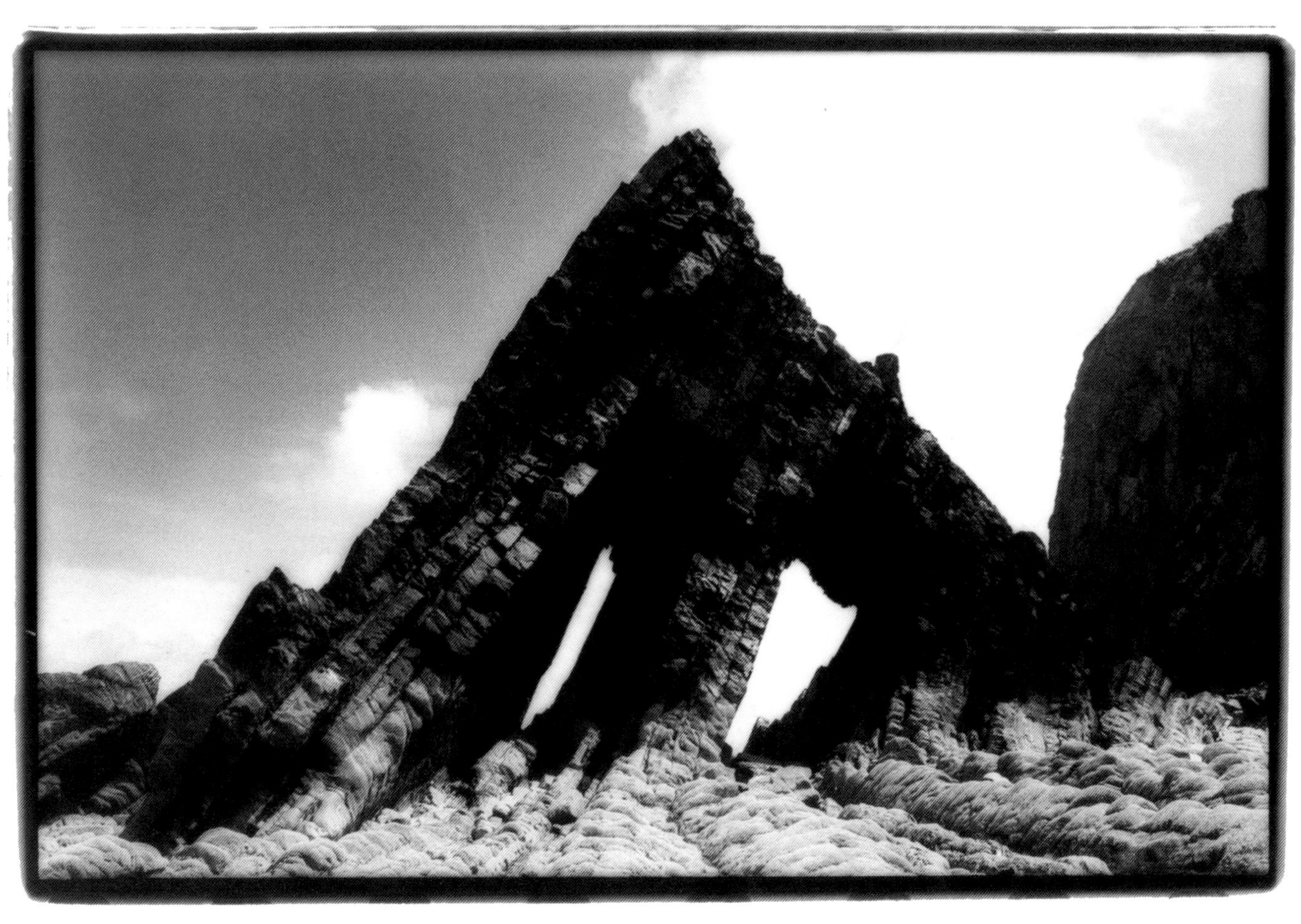

18
Blackchurch Rock I
Mouthmill, Hartland

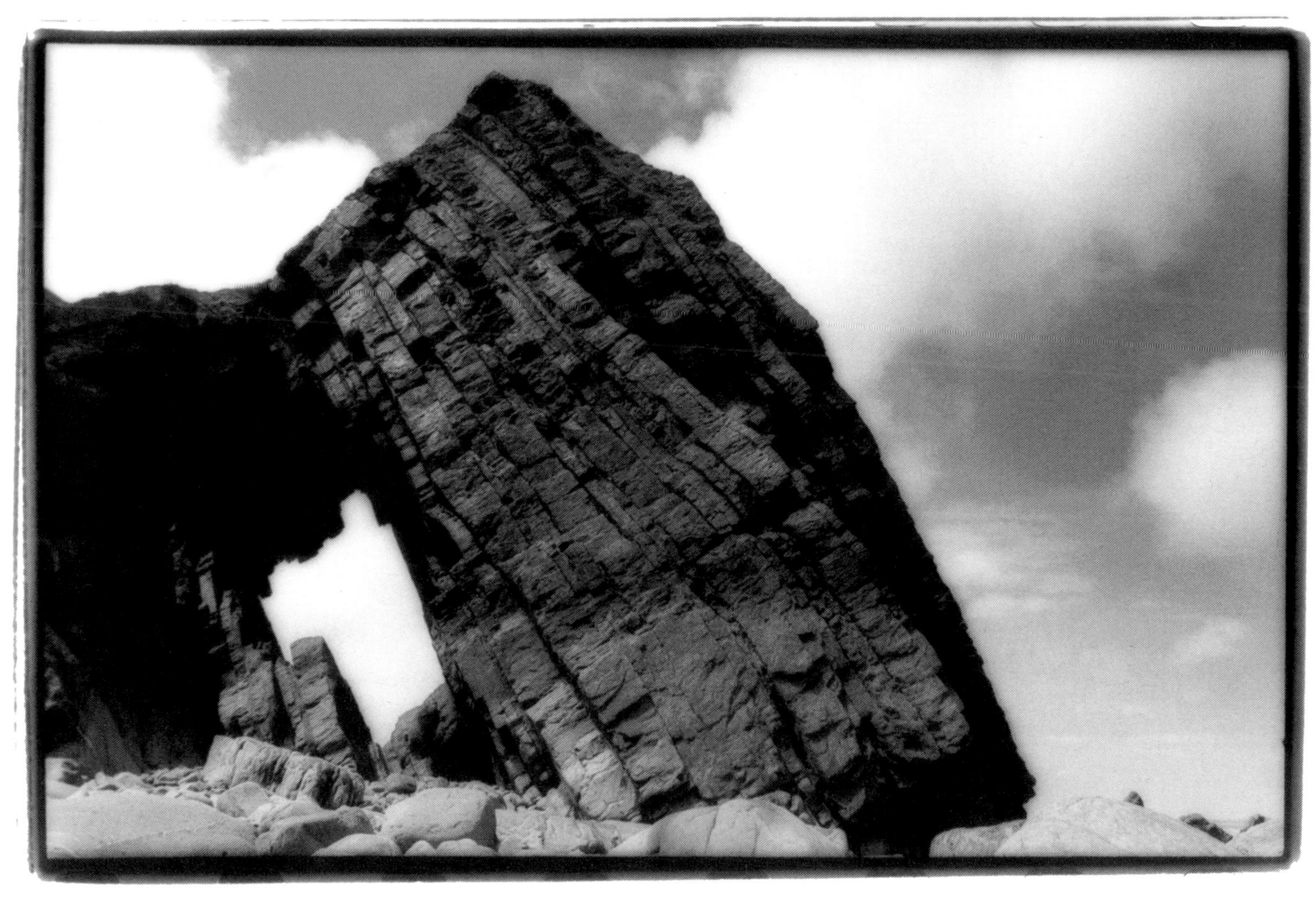

19
Blackchurch Rock II
Mouthmill, Hartland

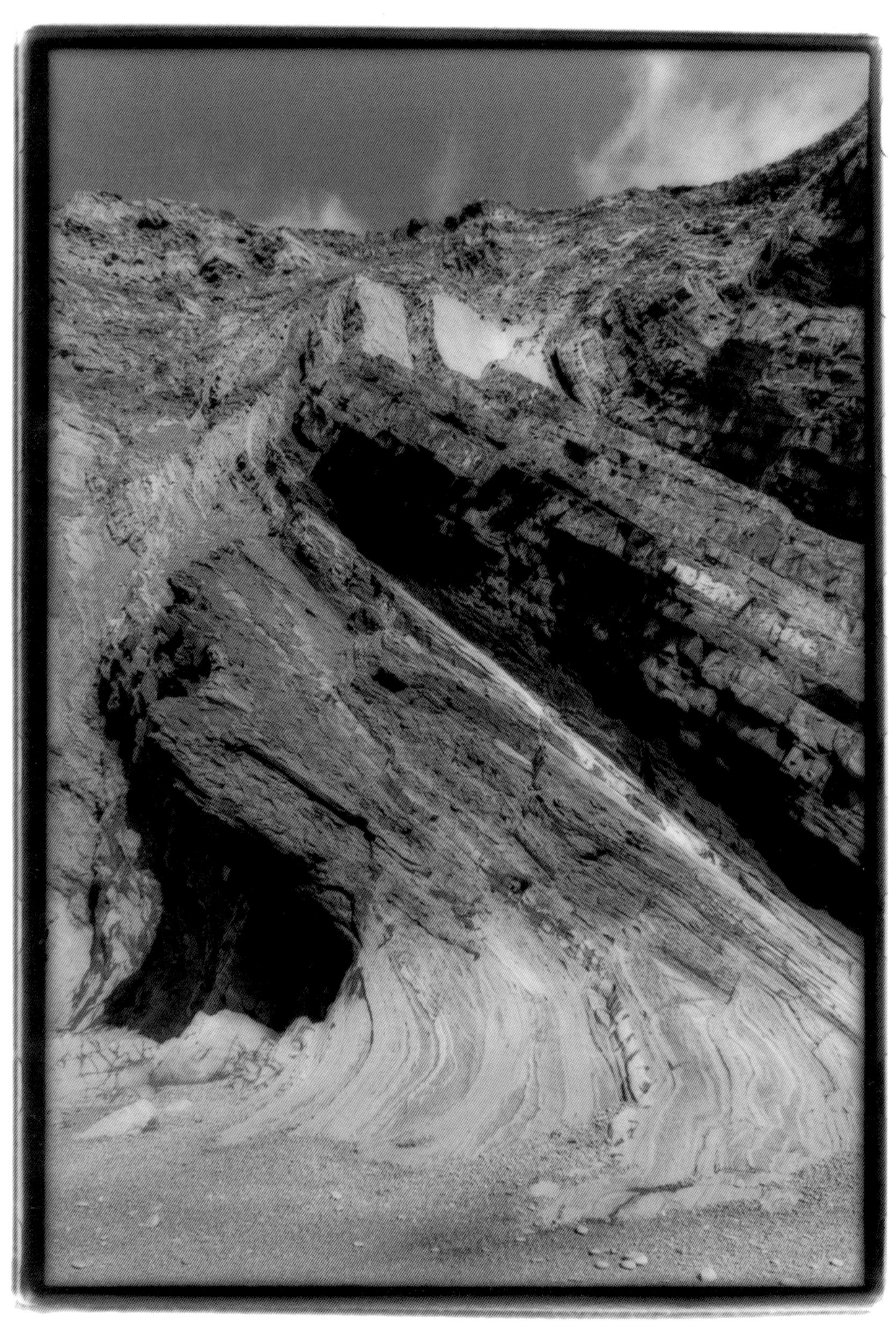

20
Cliffs at Warren
Near Hartland Quay

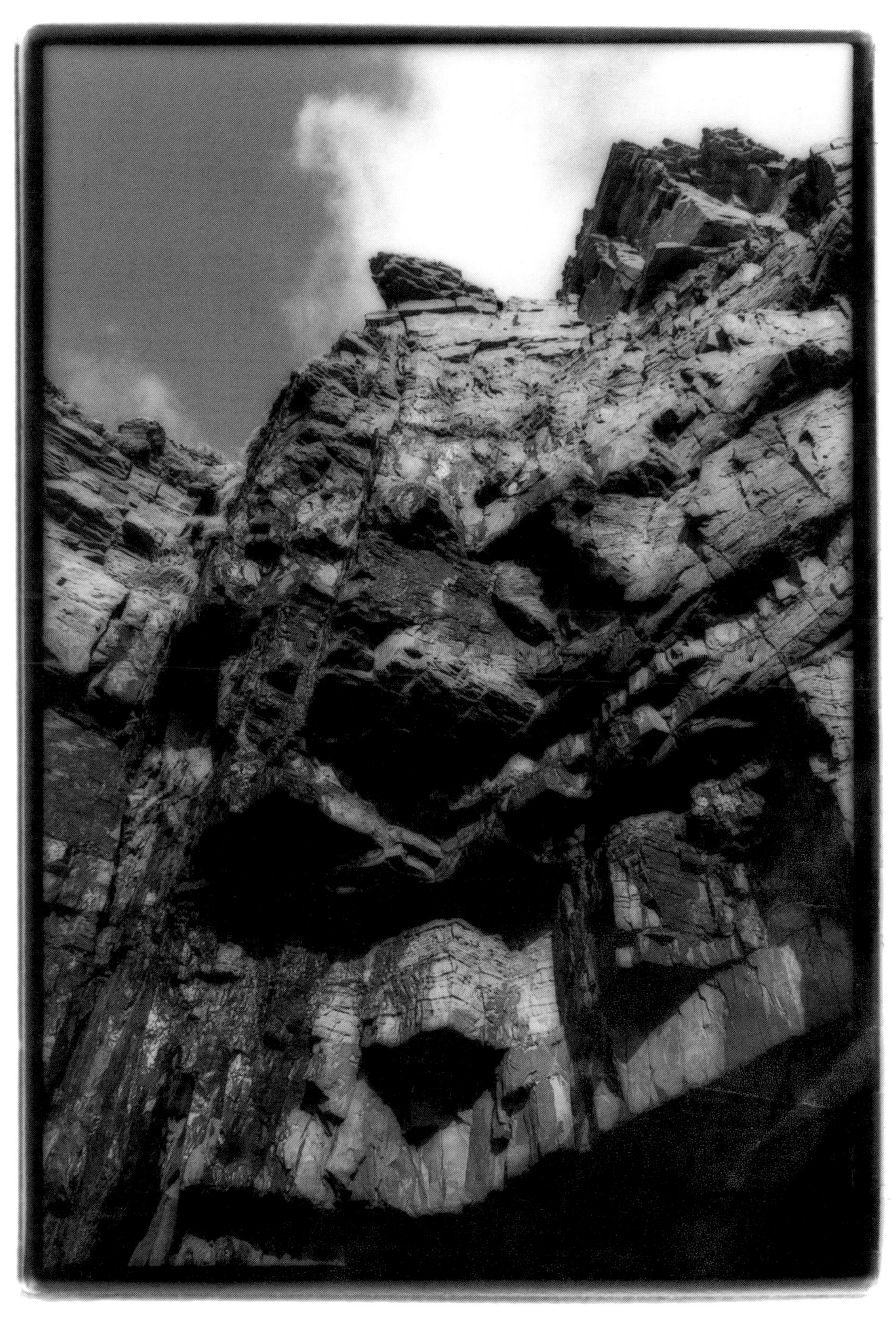

21
Overhanging cliff
Near Damehole Point, Hartland

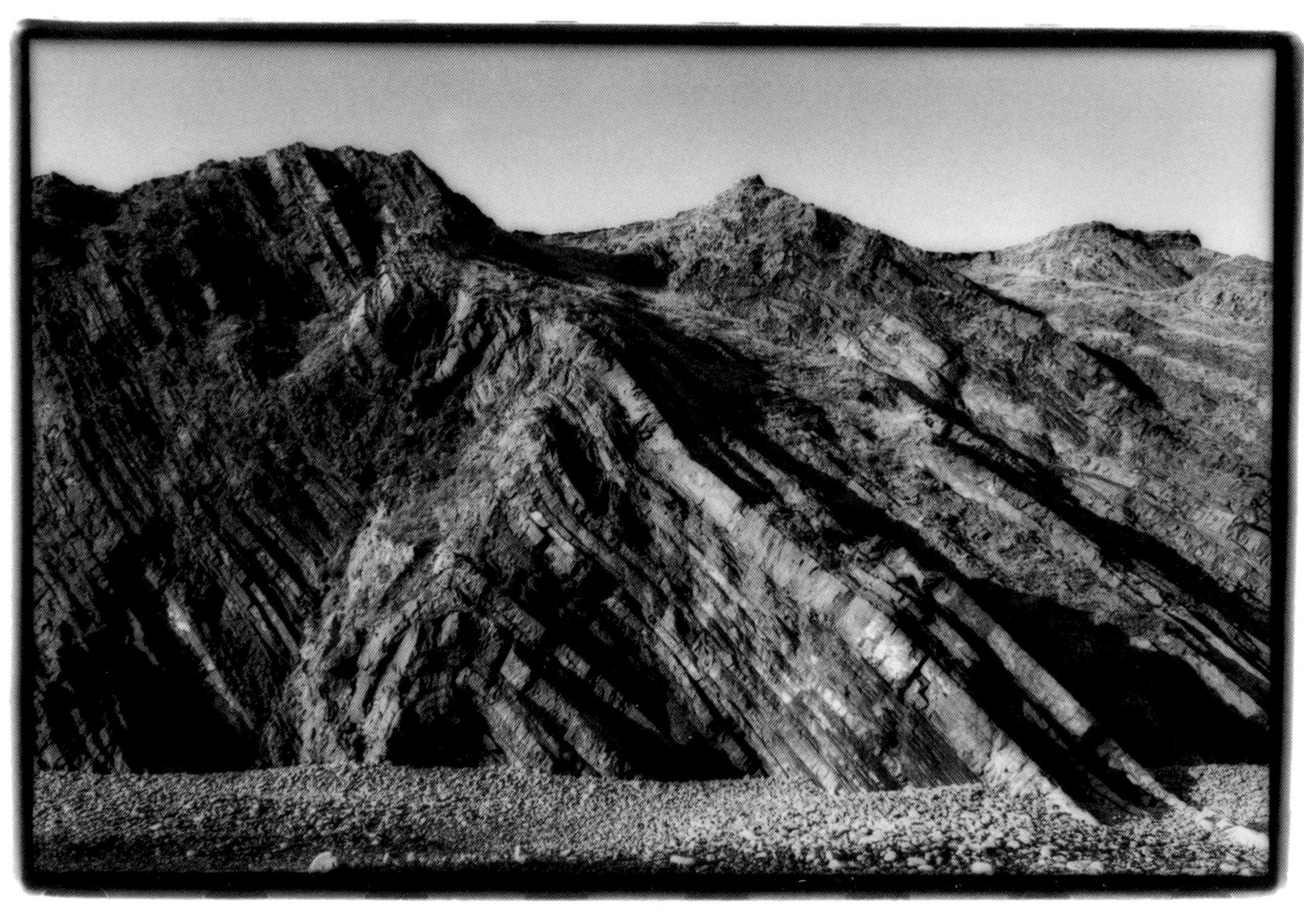

22
Speke's Mill mouth
Hartland

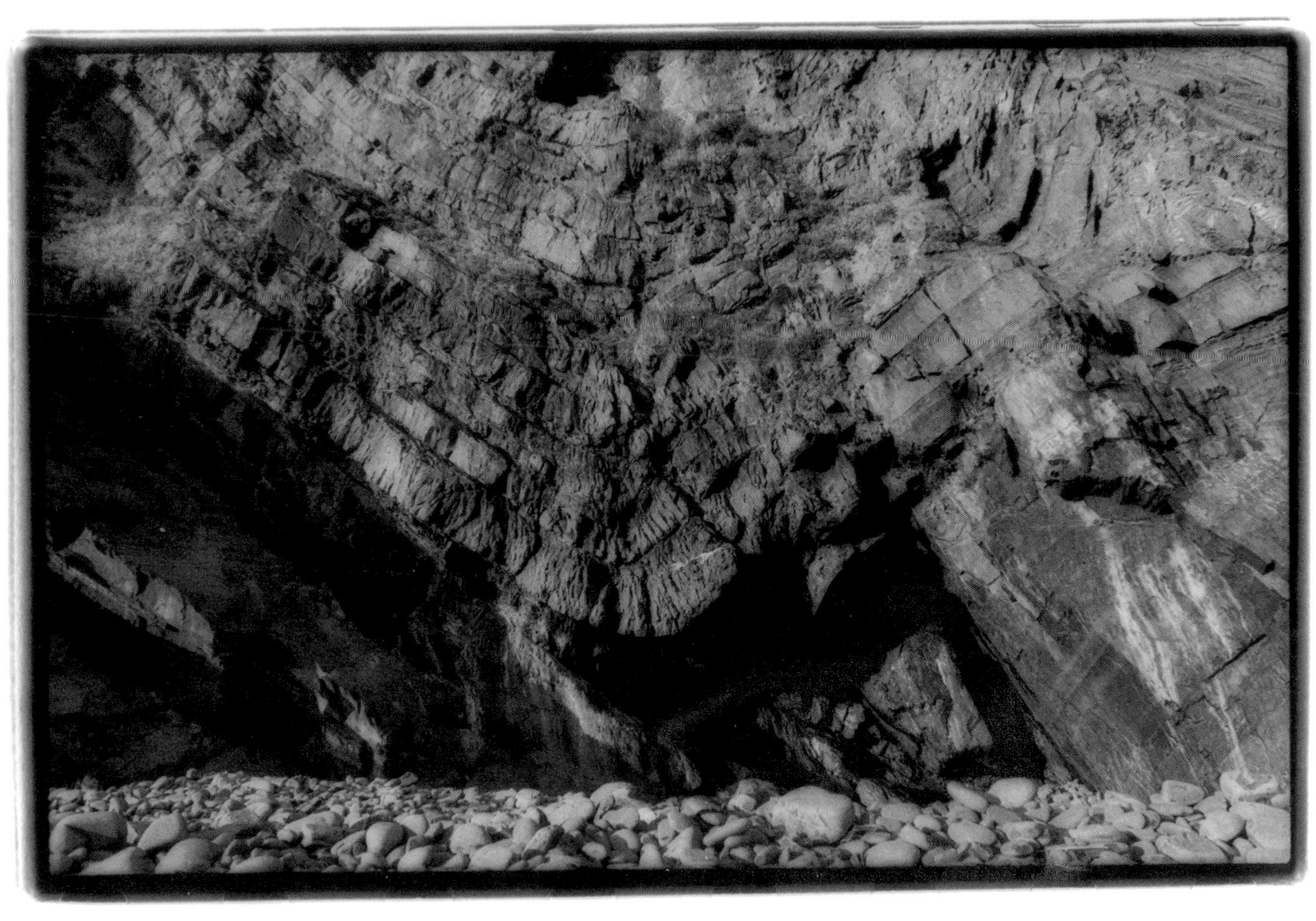

23

Folded strata

Speke's Mill mouth, Hartland

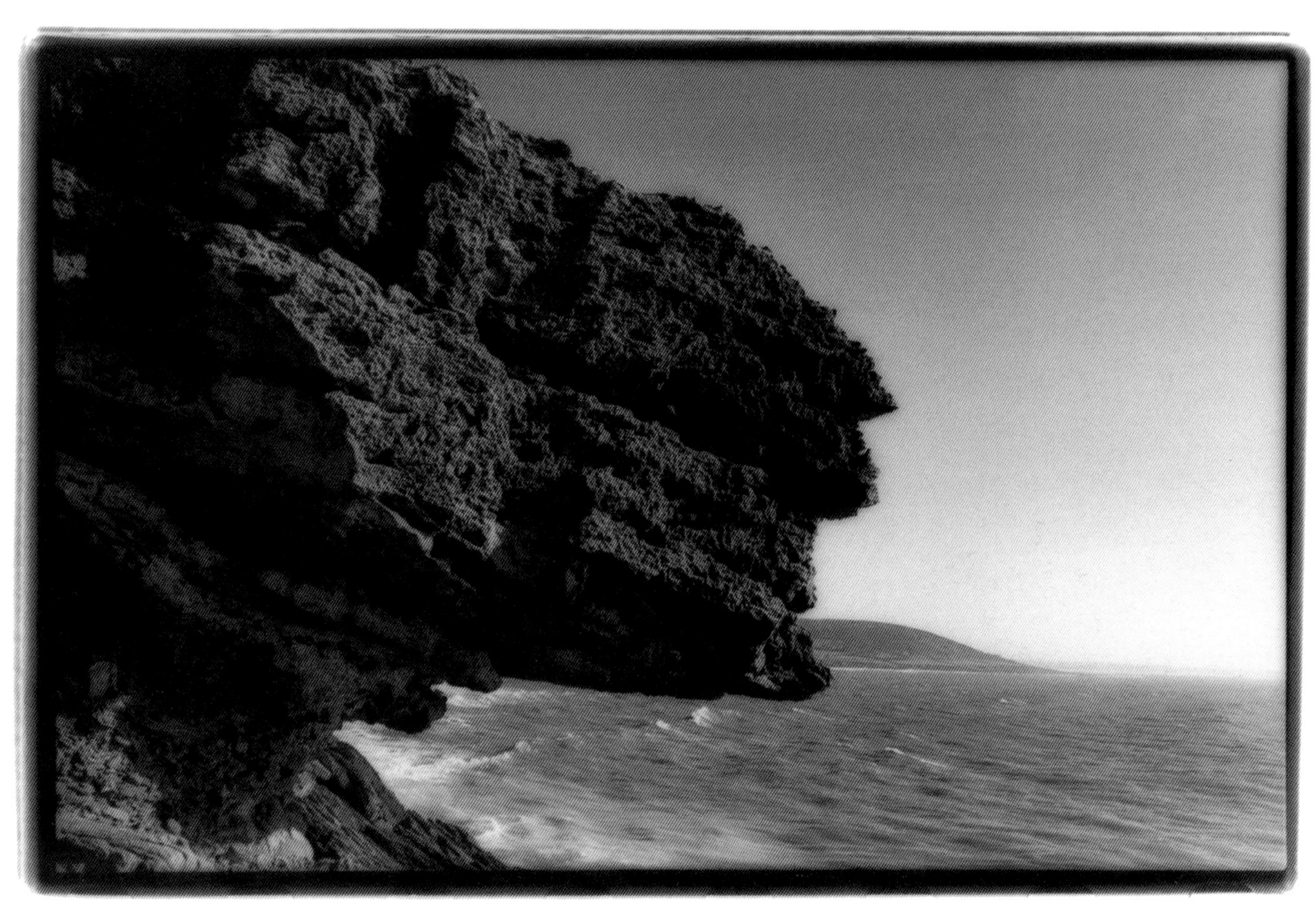

24
Baggy Point
Croyde Bay

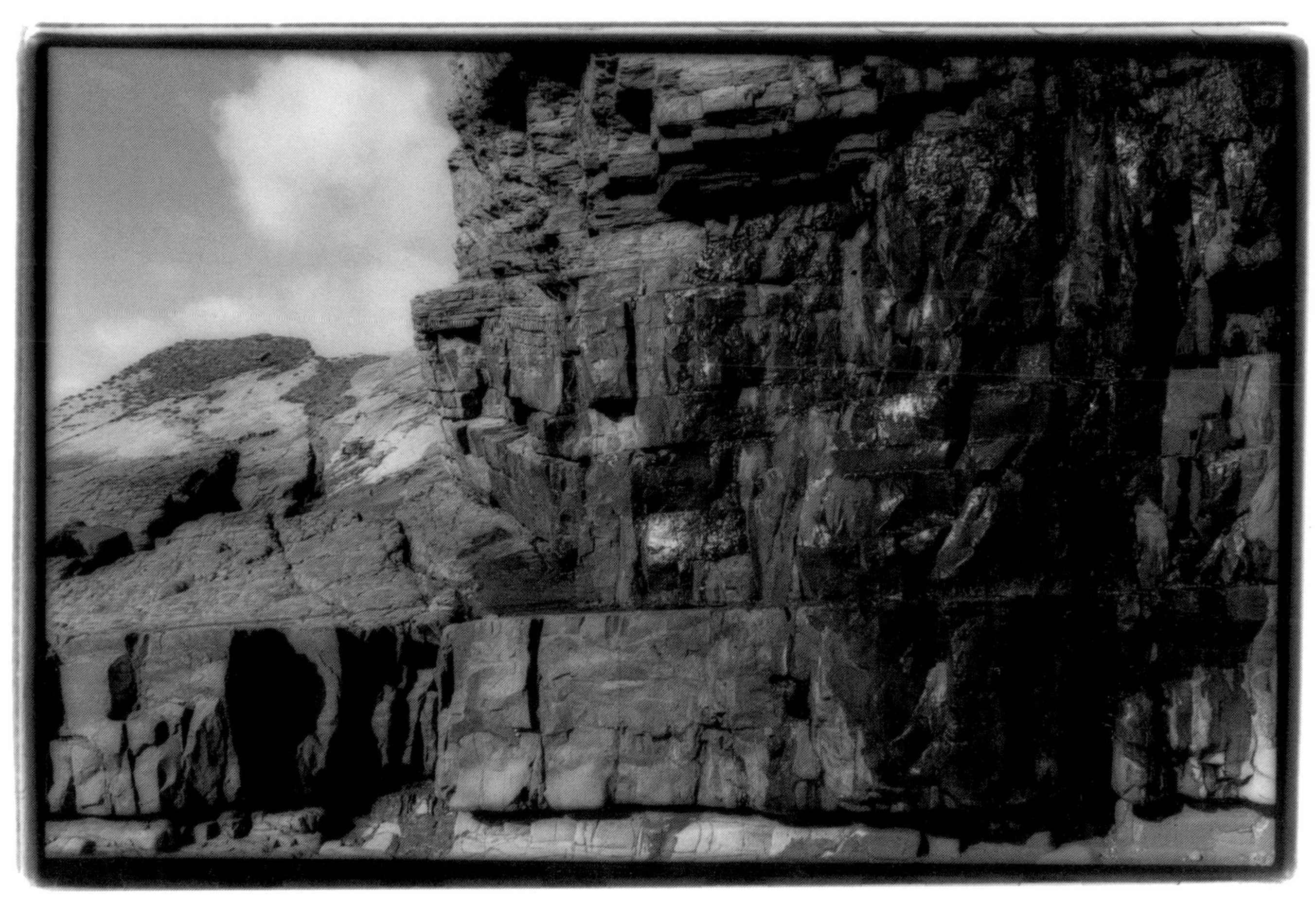

25
Cliffs at Broad Beach
Hartland

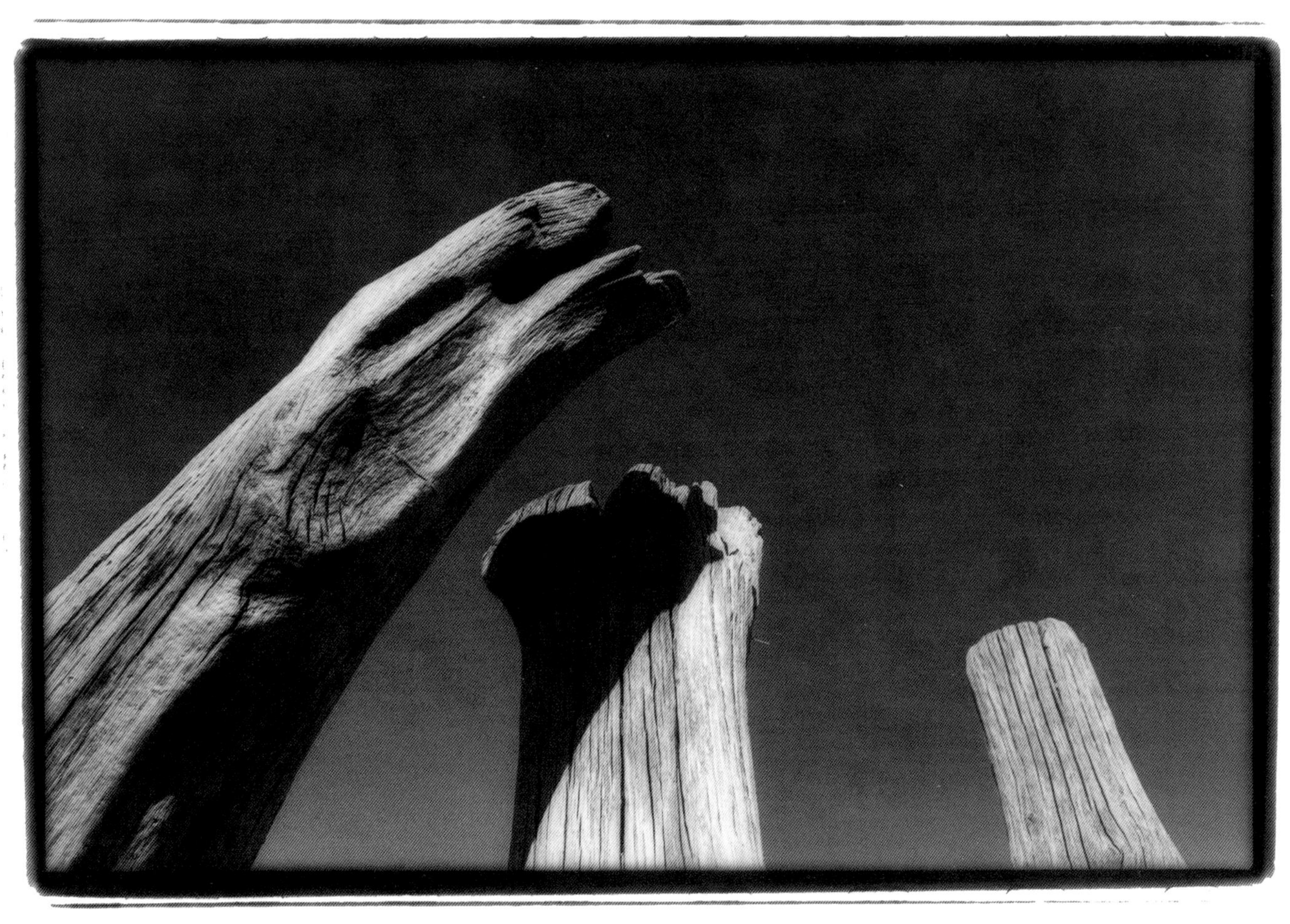

26
Weathered groyne I
Crow Point

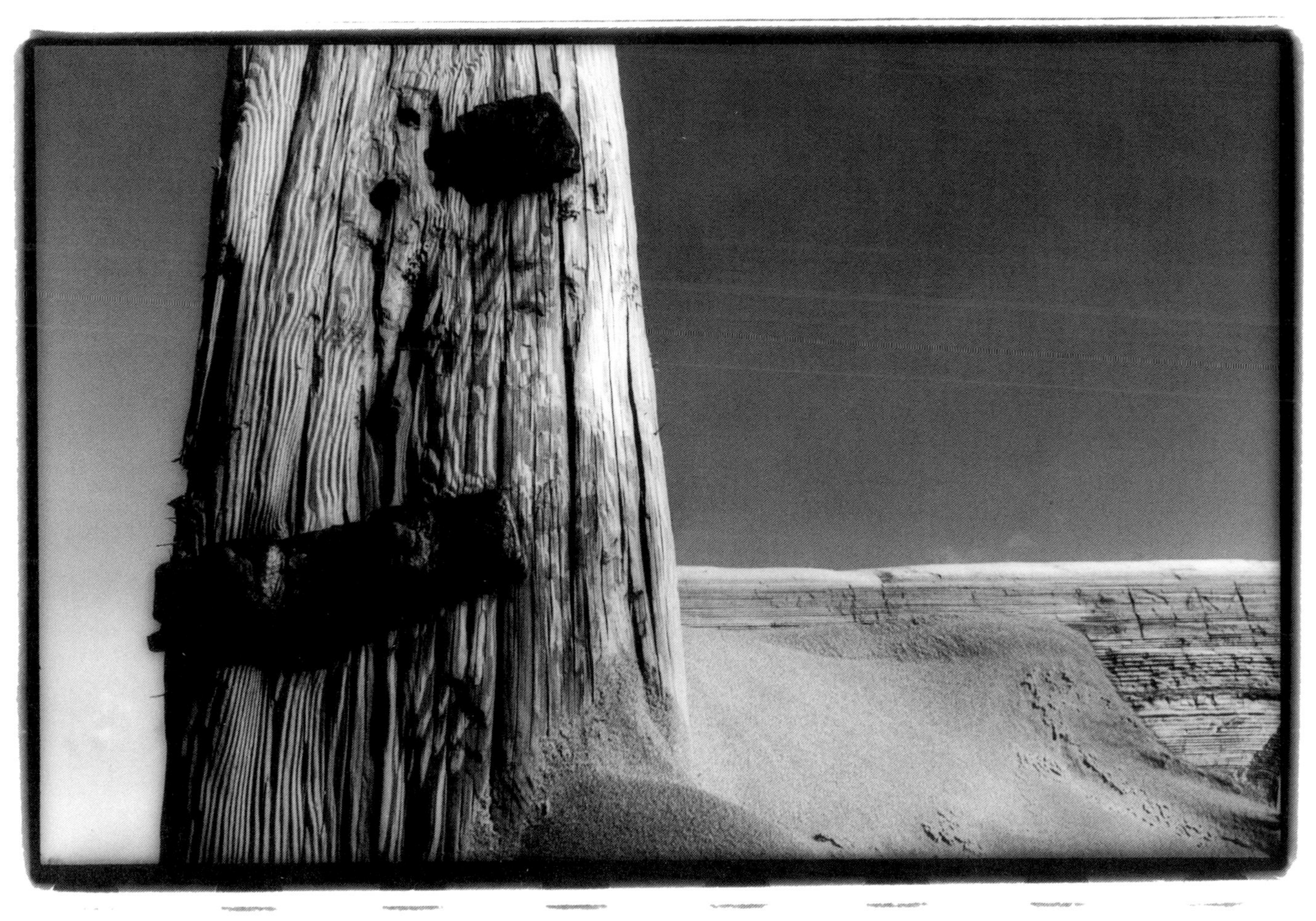

27
Weathered groyne II
Crow Point

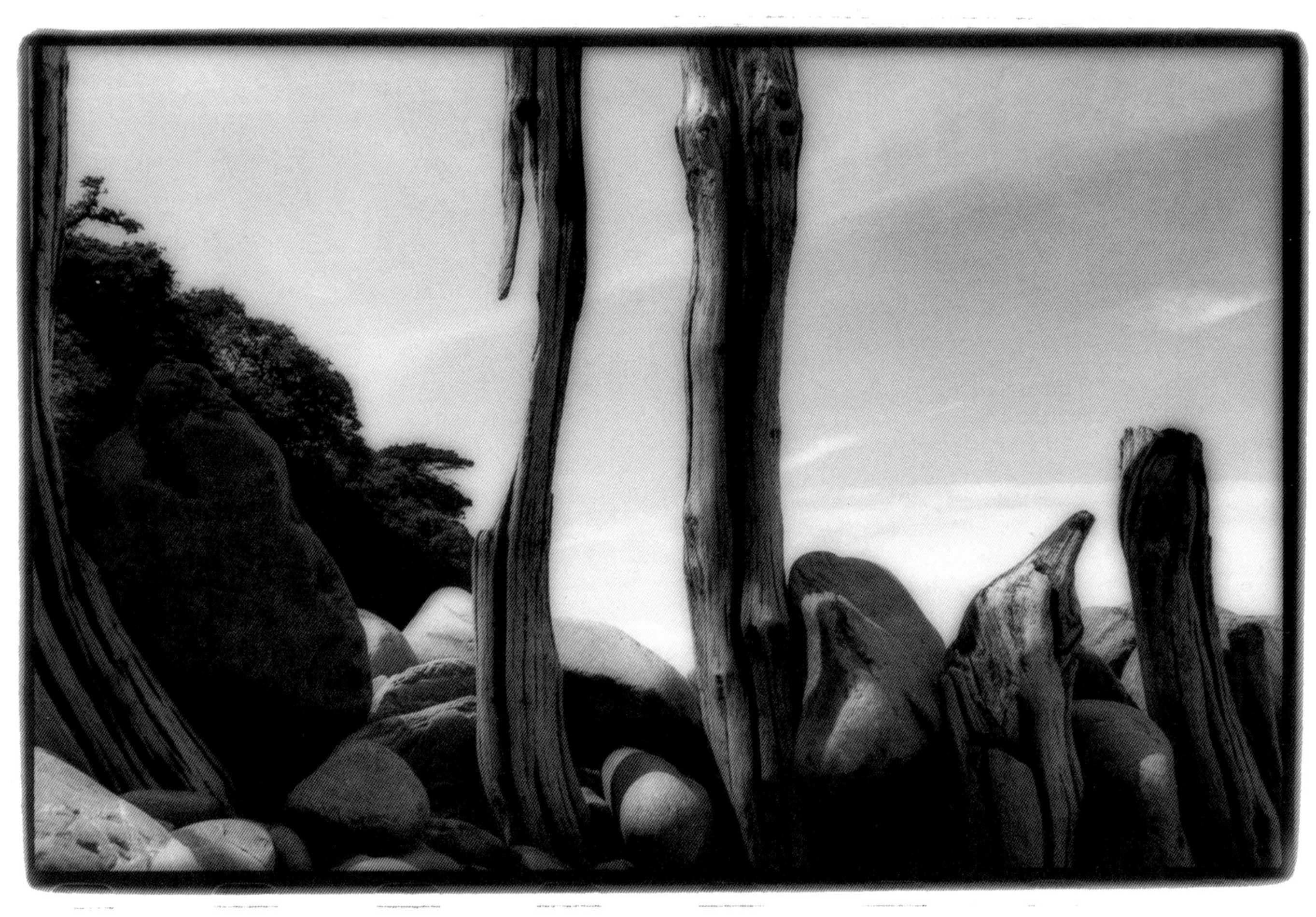

28

Last remnant of groyne

Glenthorne Beach, Exmoor

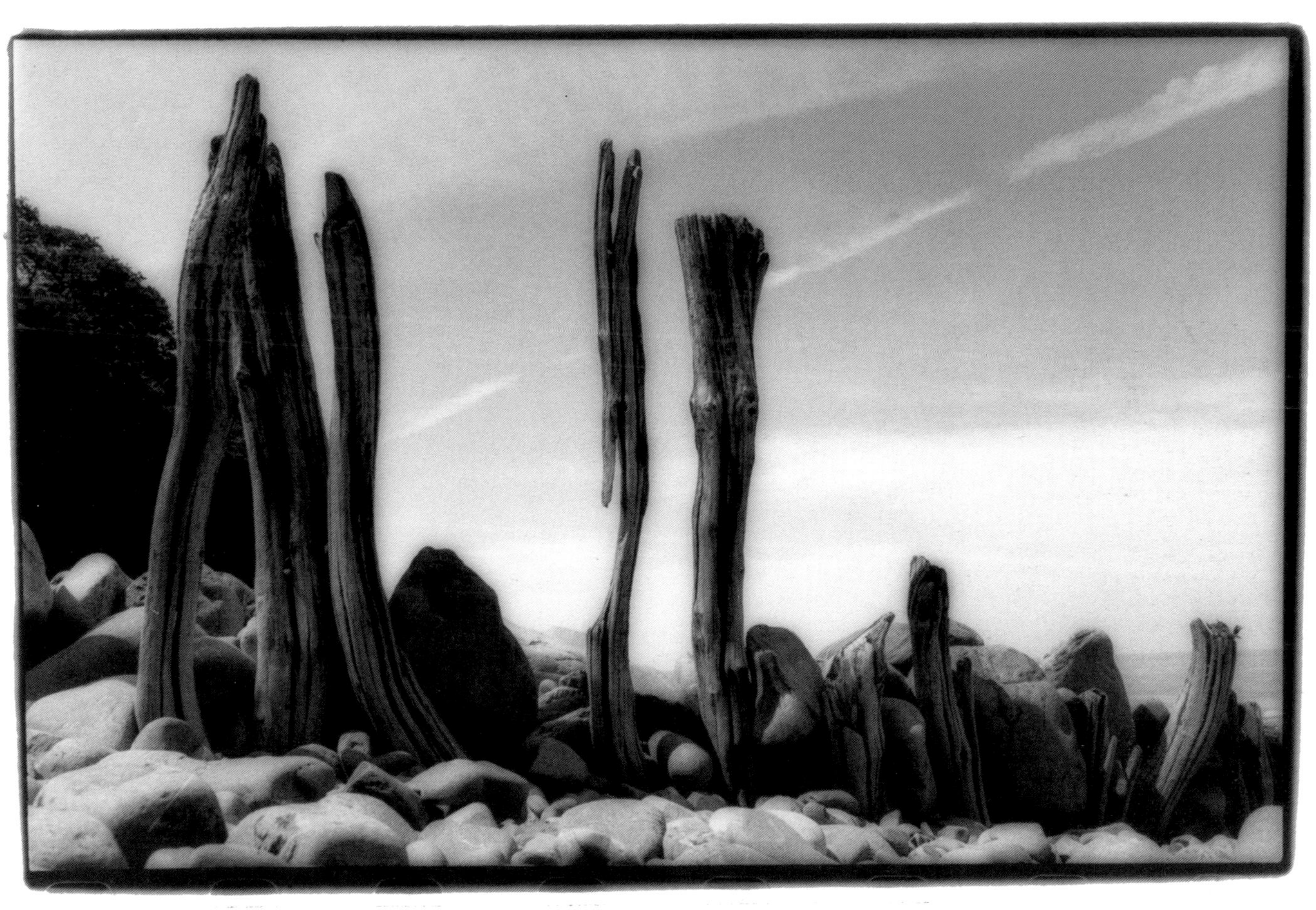

29
Weathered groyne III
Glenthorne Beach, Exmoor

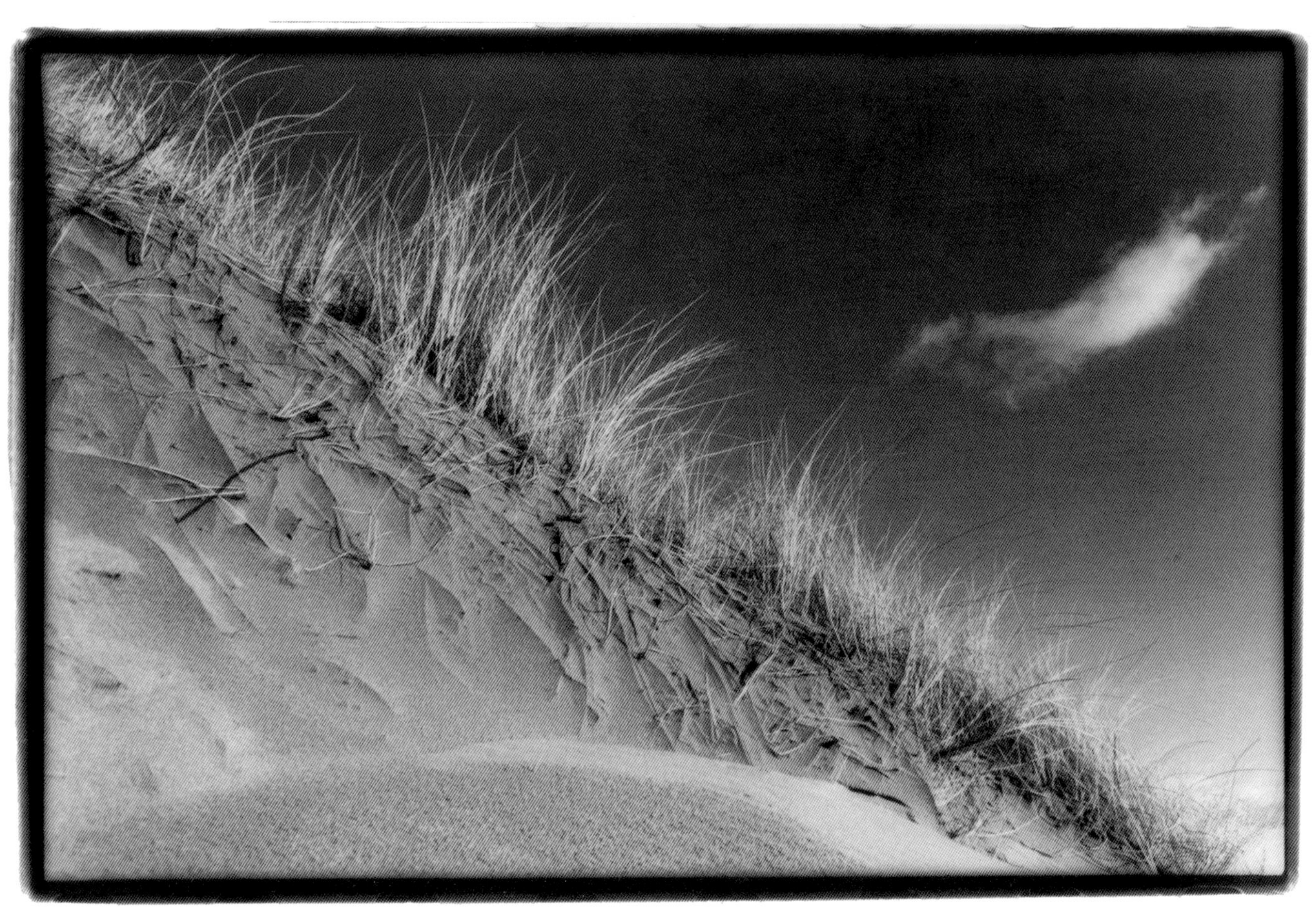

30
Marram grass
Braunton Burrows

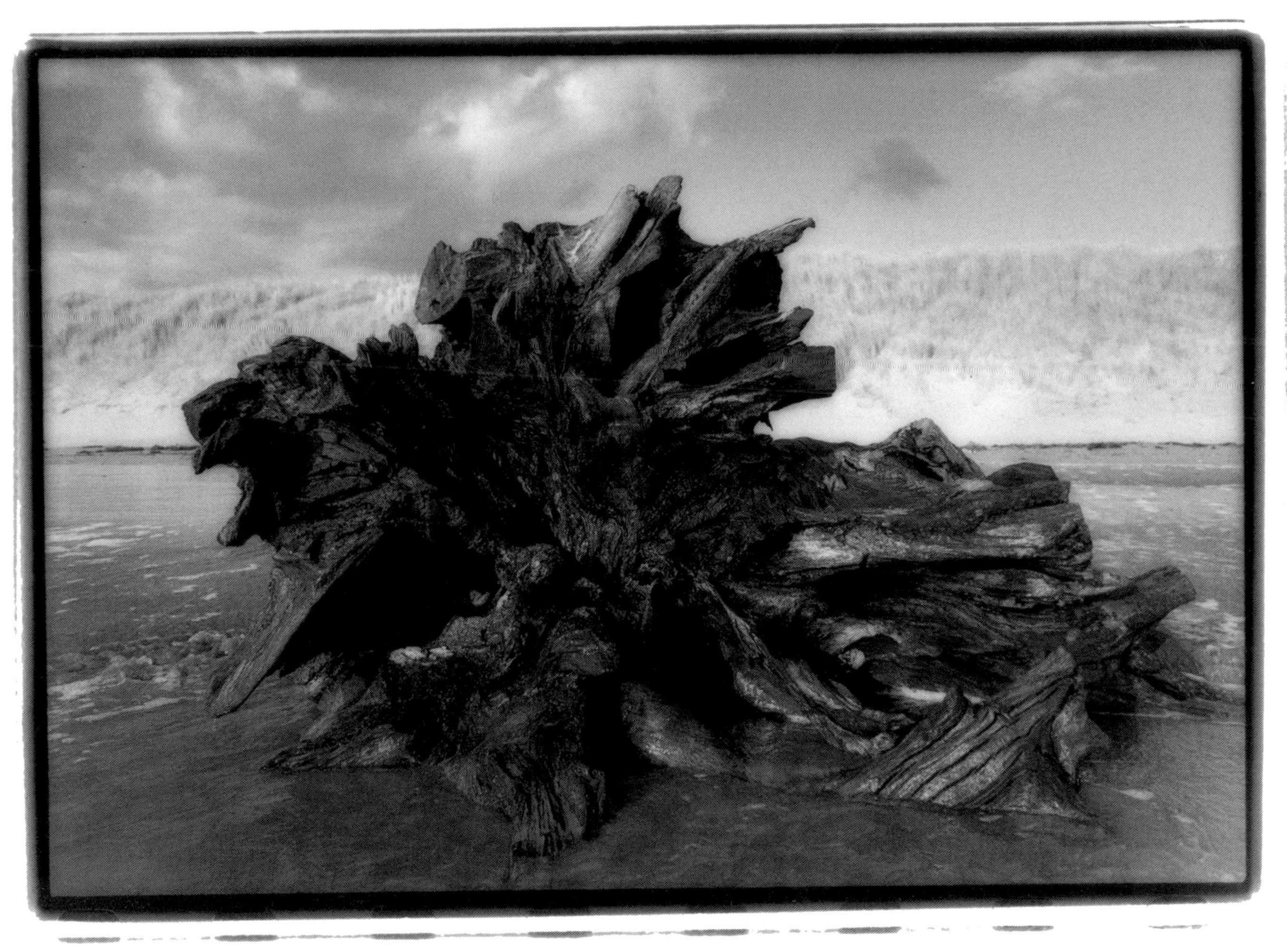

31
Driftwood
Saunton Sands

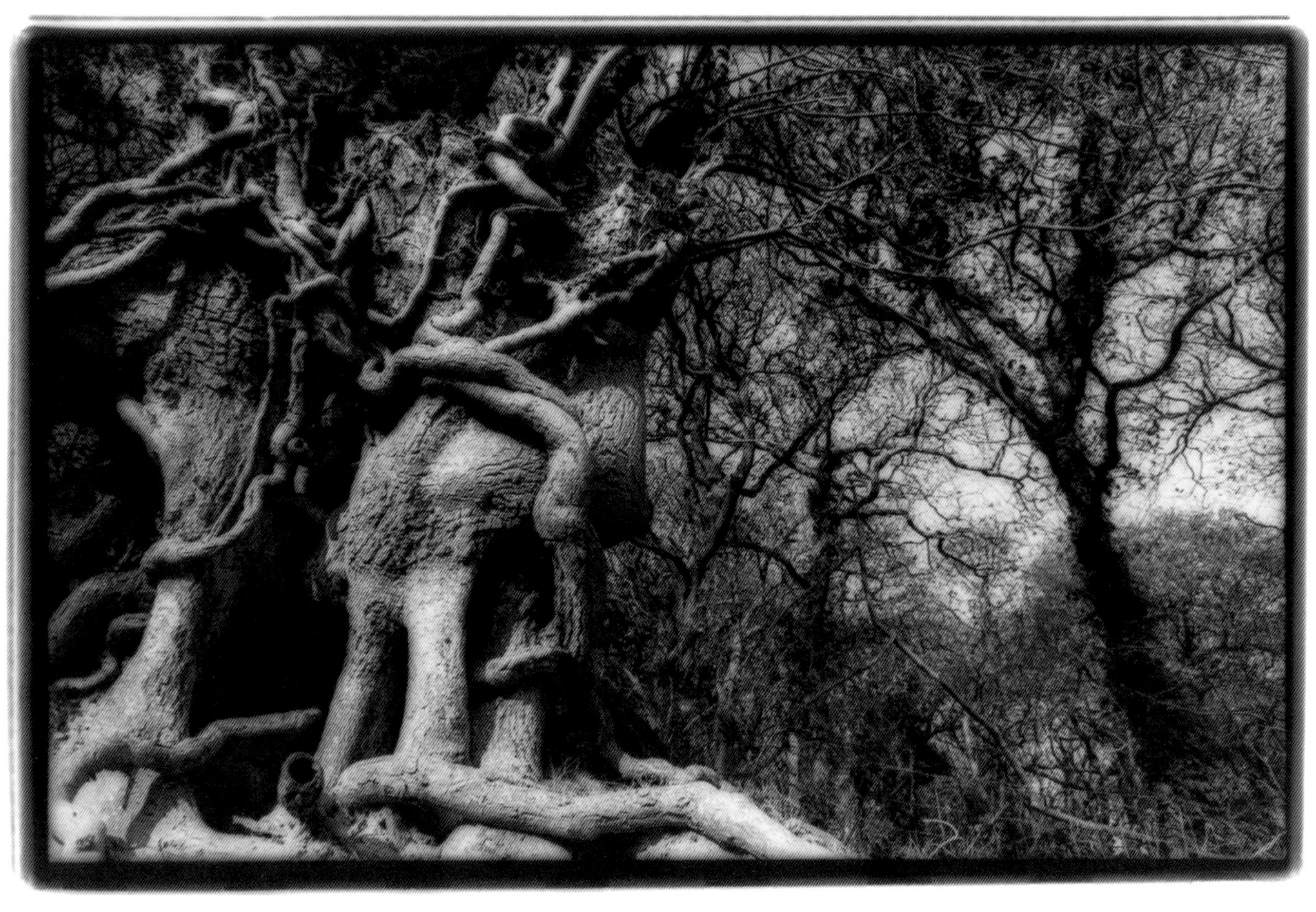

32
Park Wood
Near Ash Barton

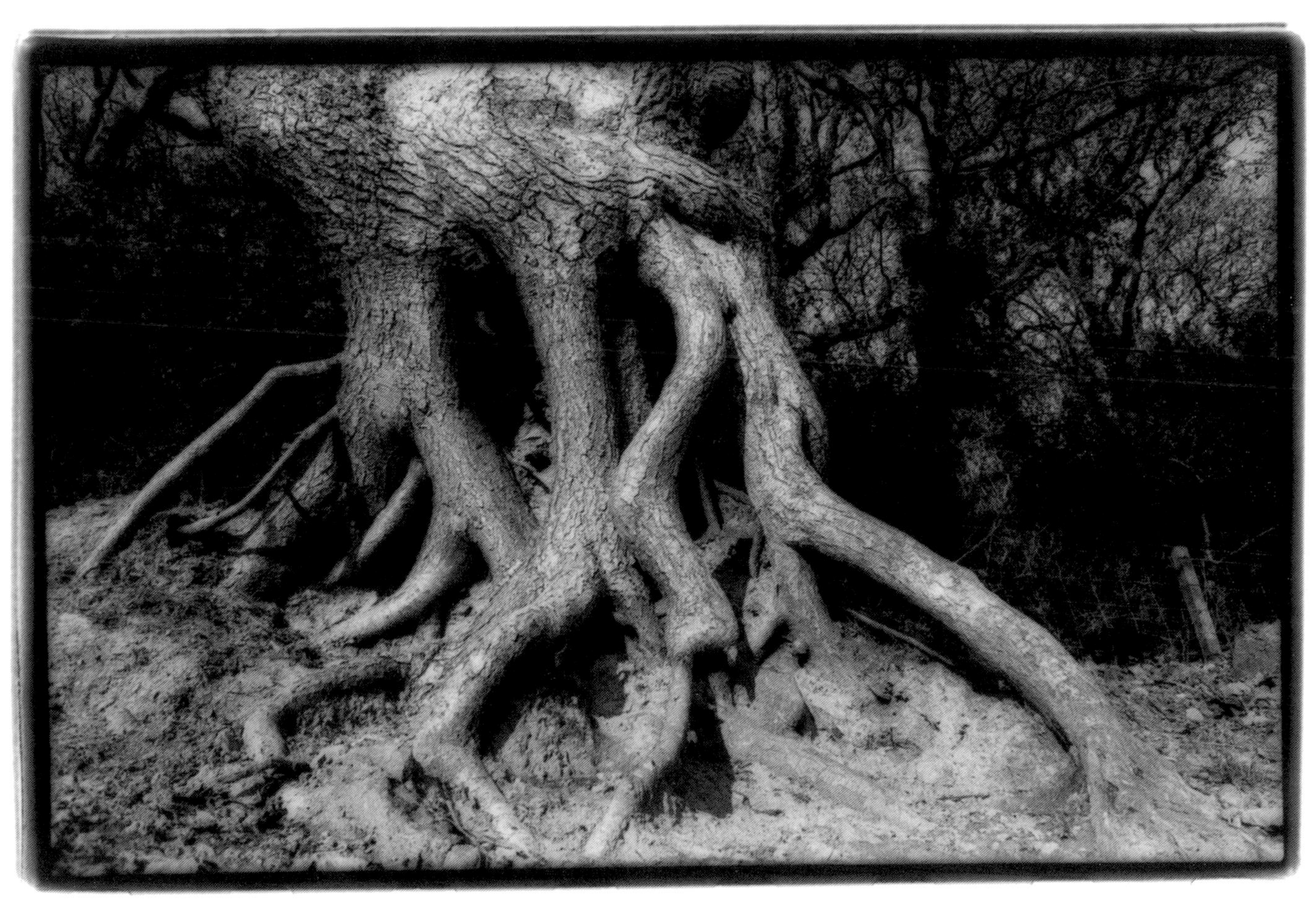

33
Exposed oak roots
Luscott, Barton

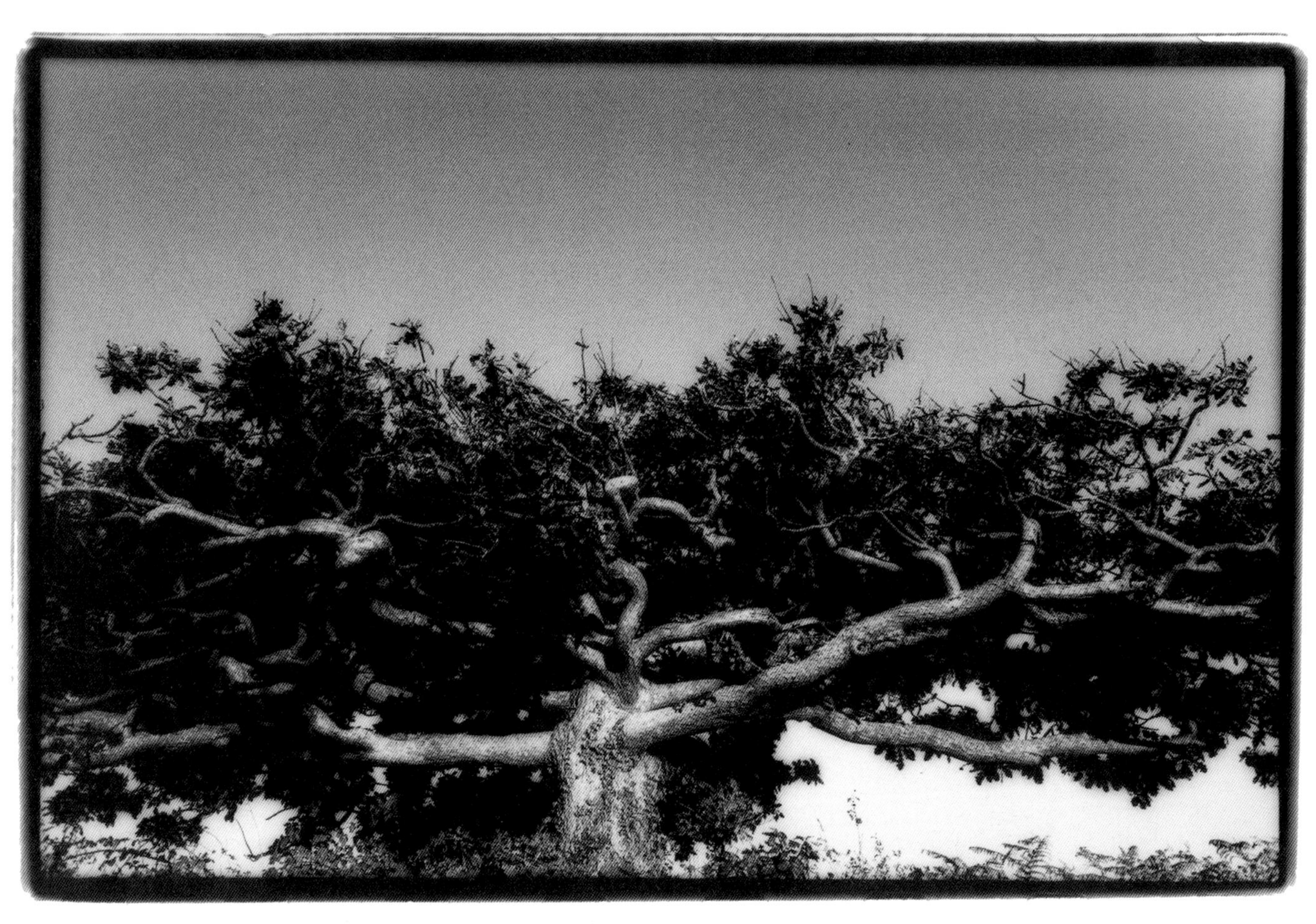

34
Gnarled oak
Near Georgeham

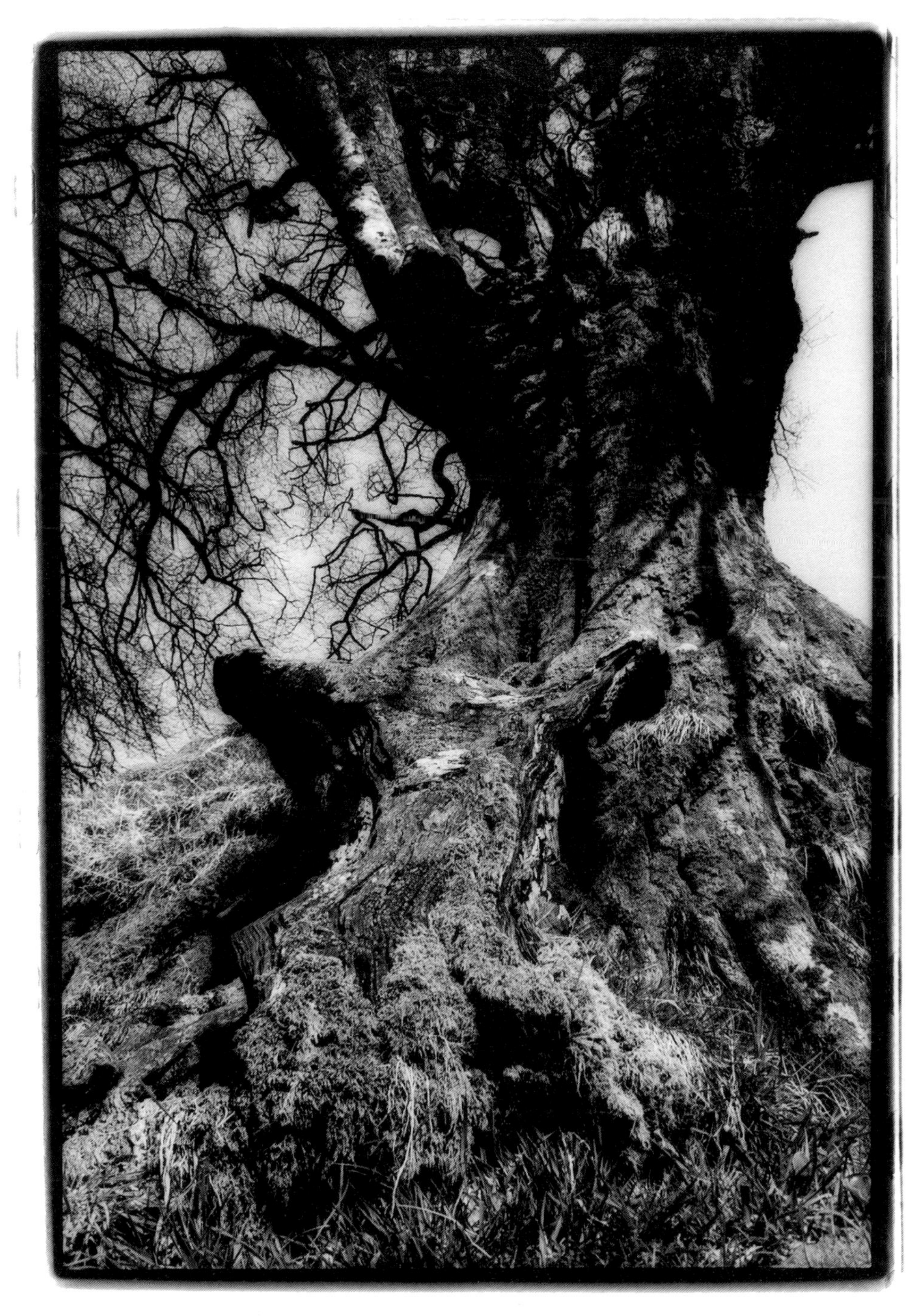

35
Buttress roots
Higher Knaplock, Exmoor

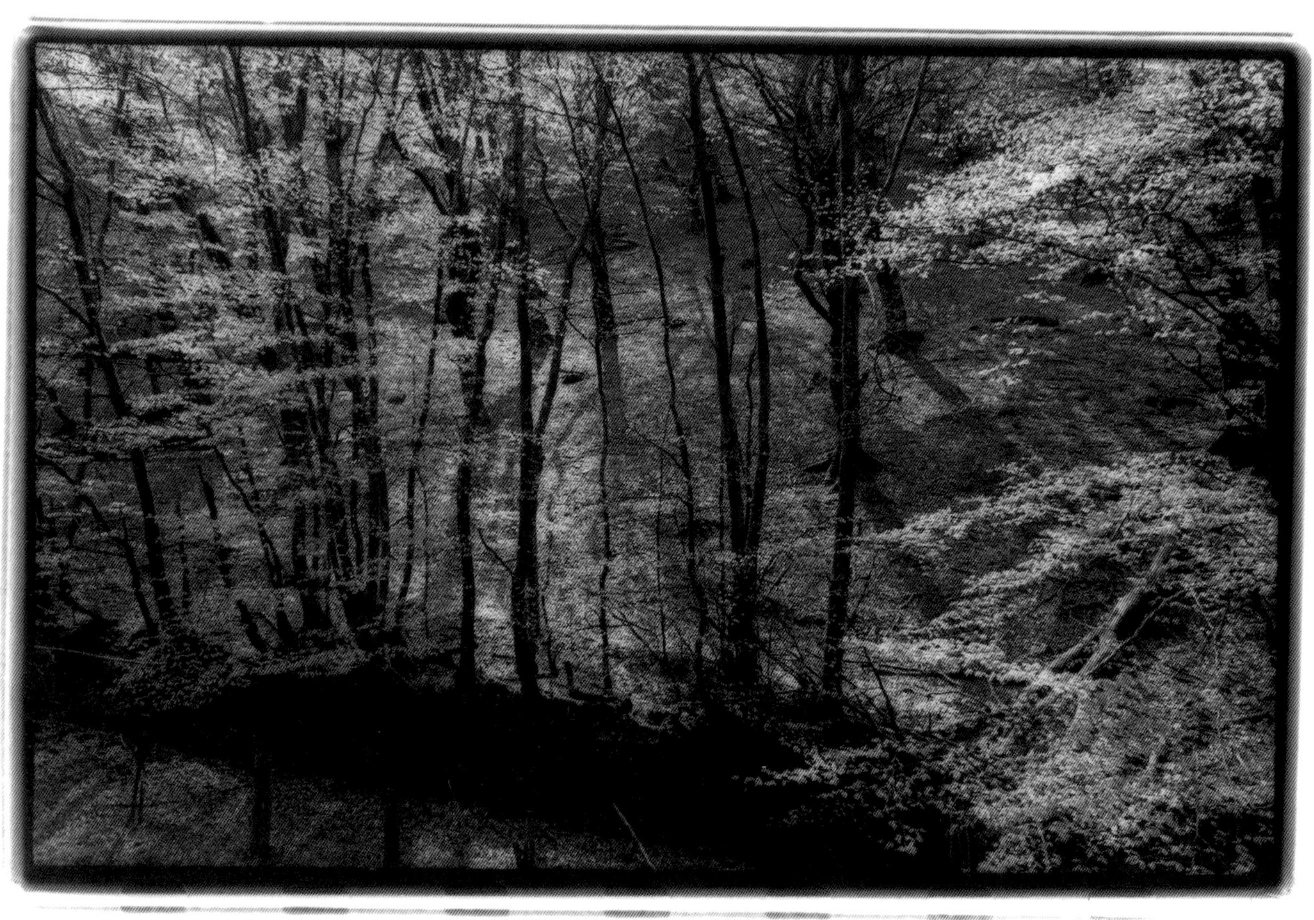

36
Knaplock Wood
Barle Valley, Exmoor

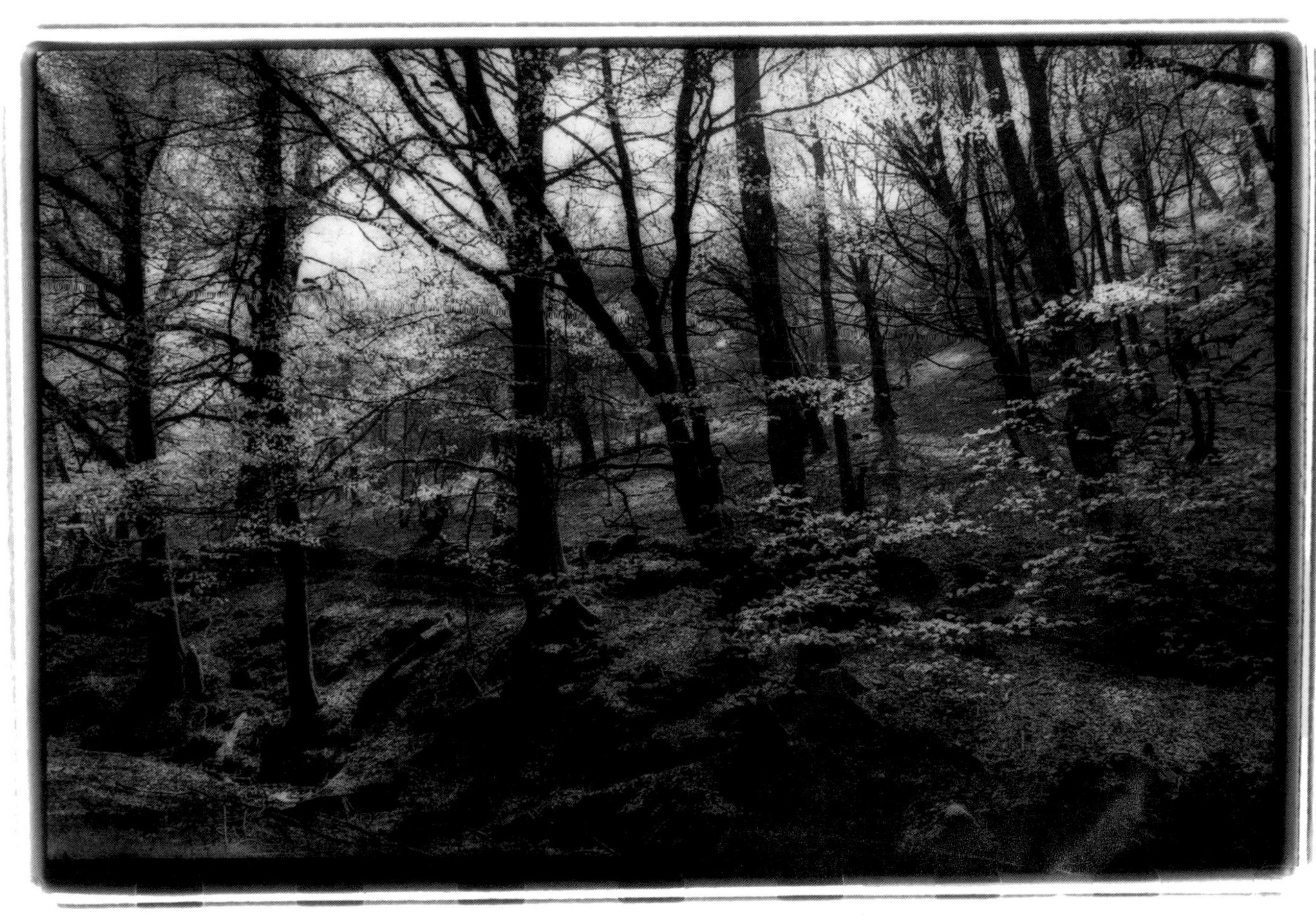

37
North Barton Wood
Barle Valley, Exmoor

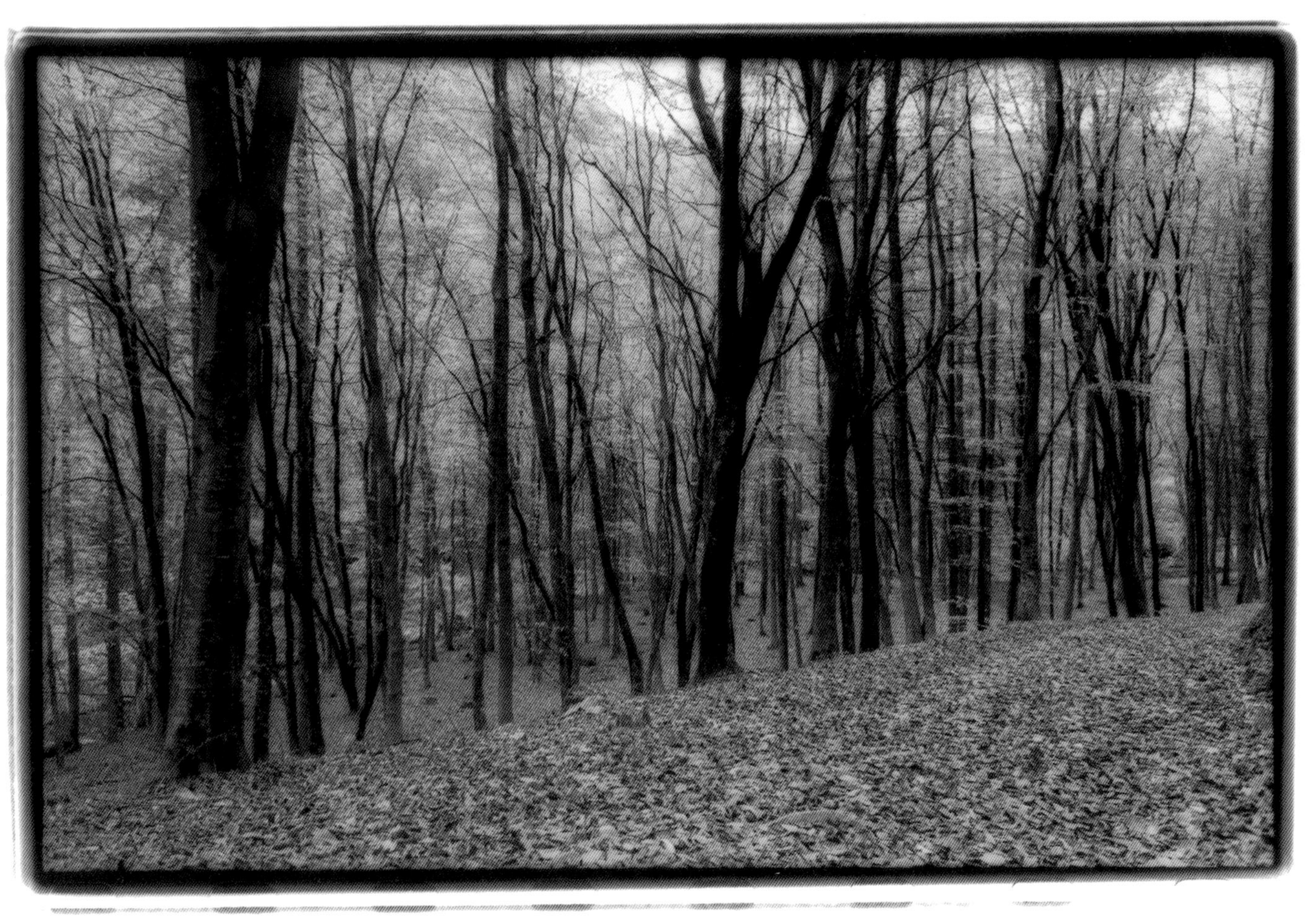

38
East Lyn Valley
Near Rockford, Exmoor

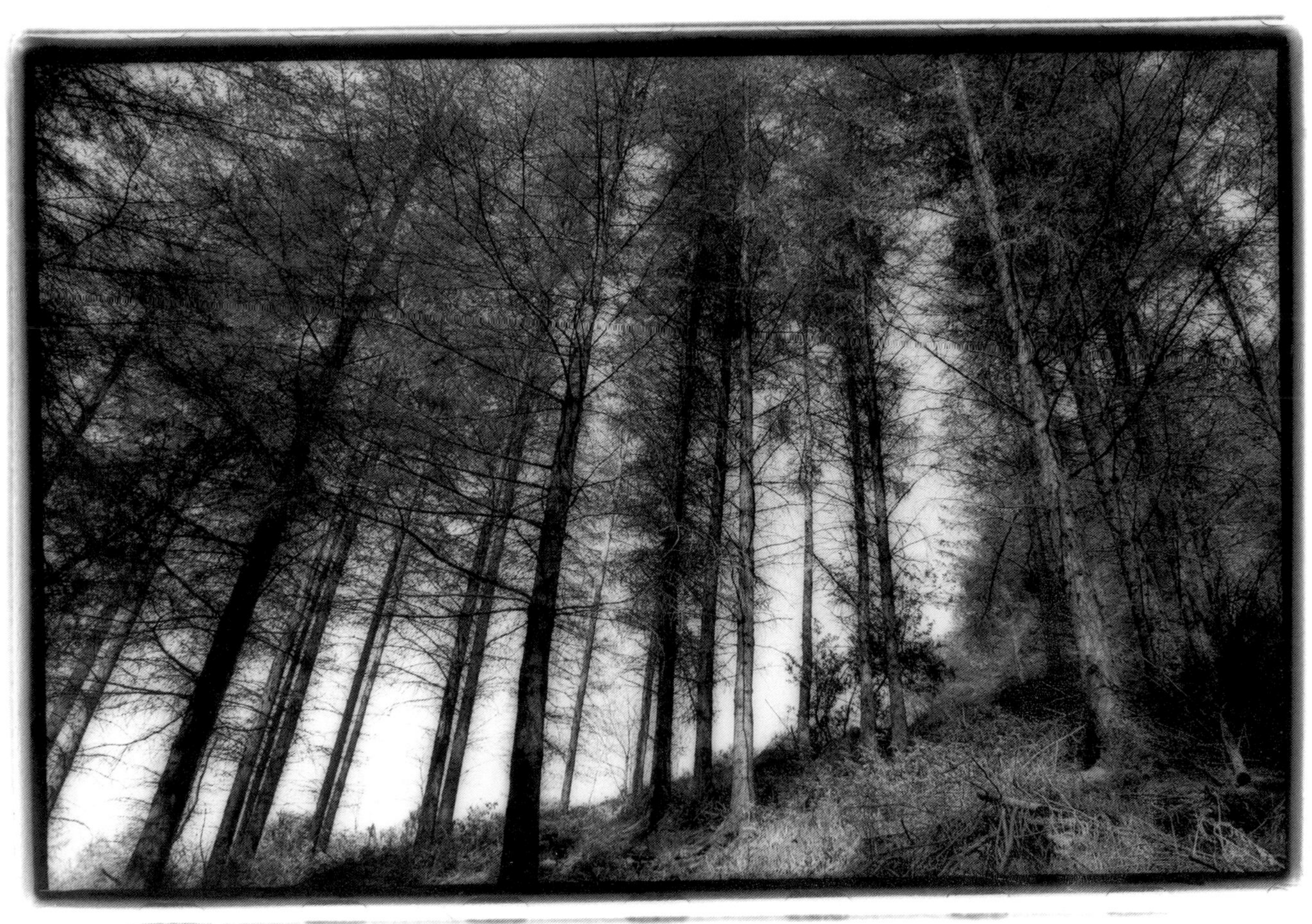

39
Larch
Barle Wood, Exmoor

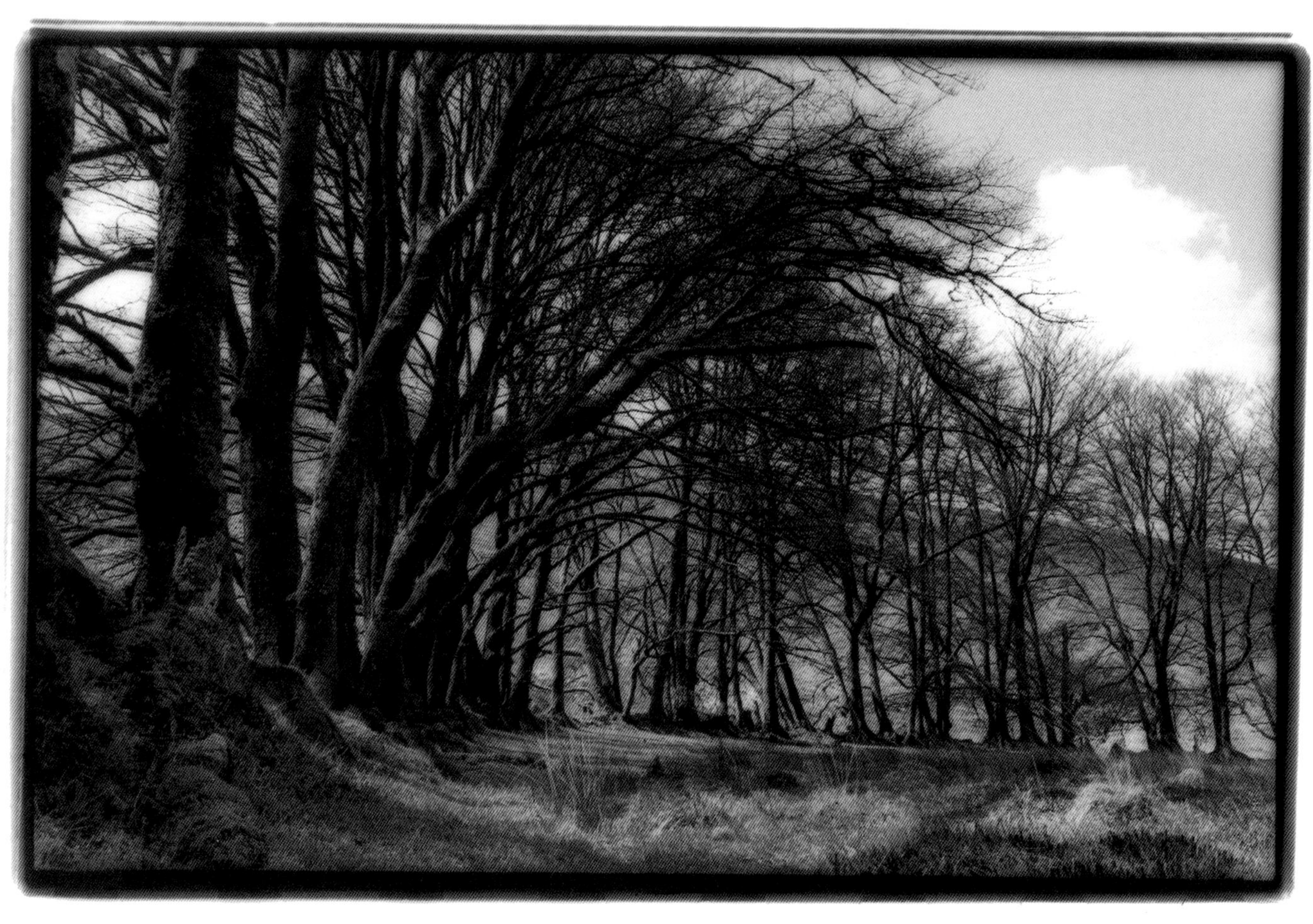

40
Below Pickedstones Farm
Exmoor

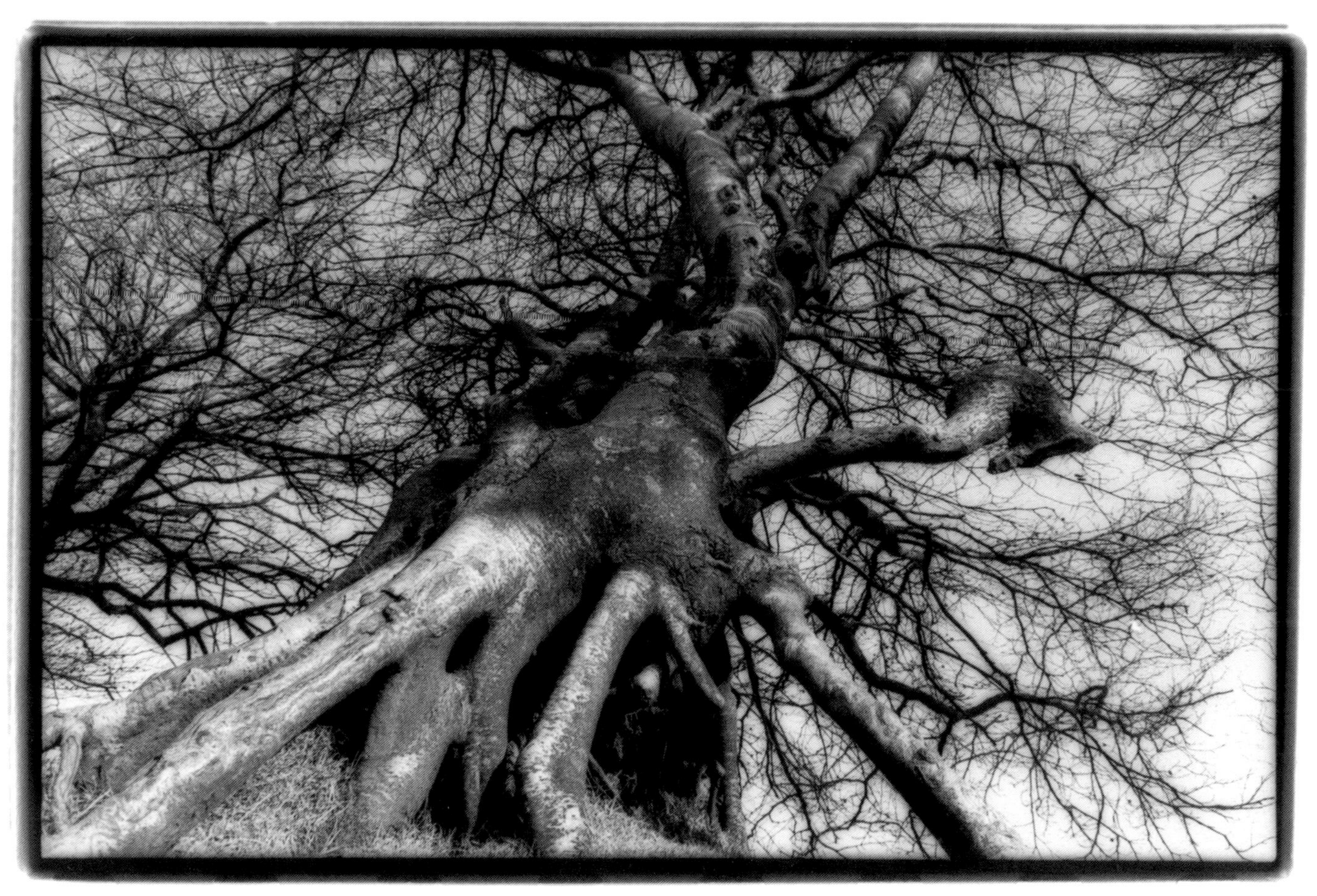

41
Near Clanger's Farm
Croyde

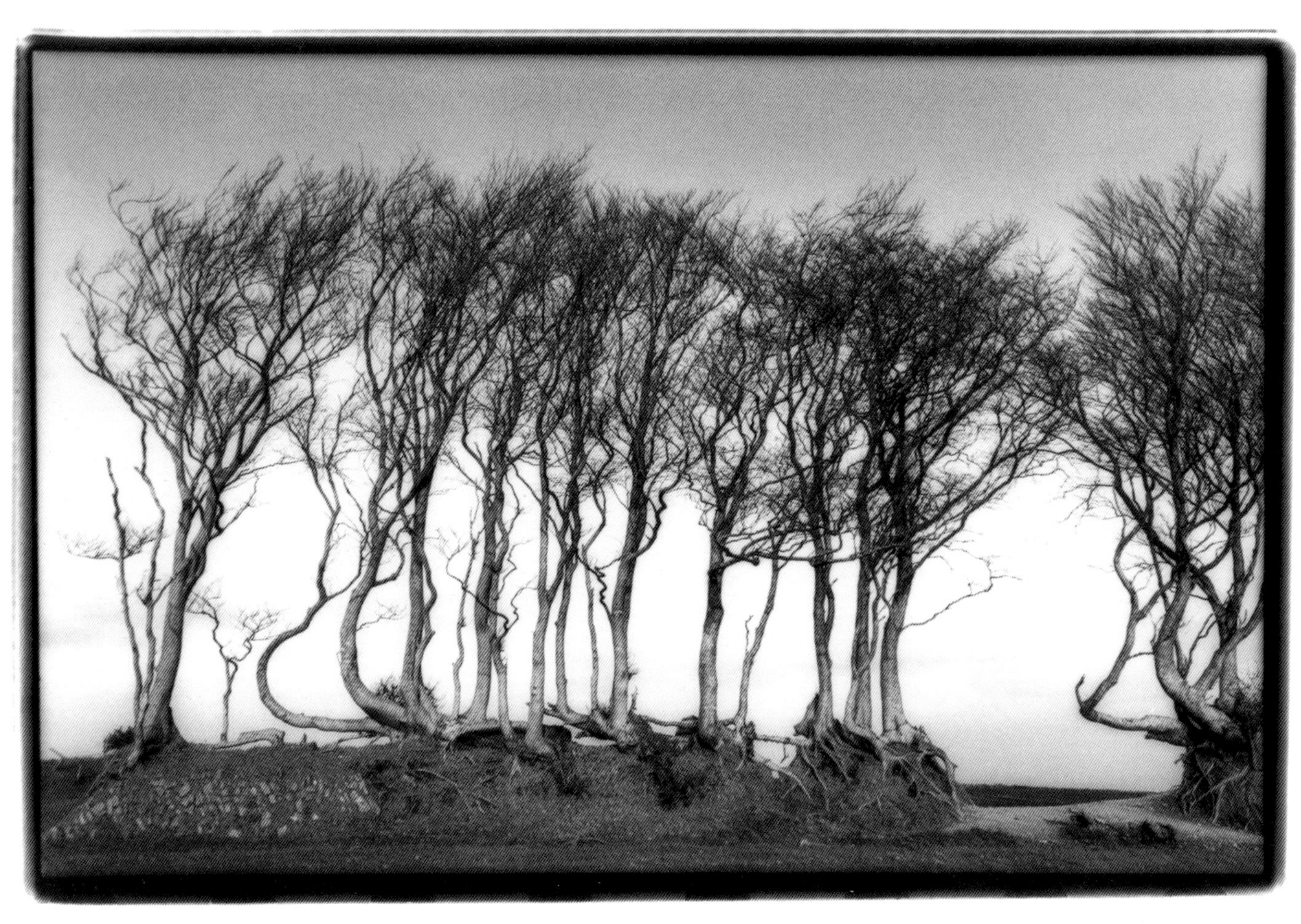

42
Caffyns Heanton Down
Exmoor

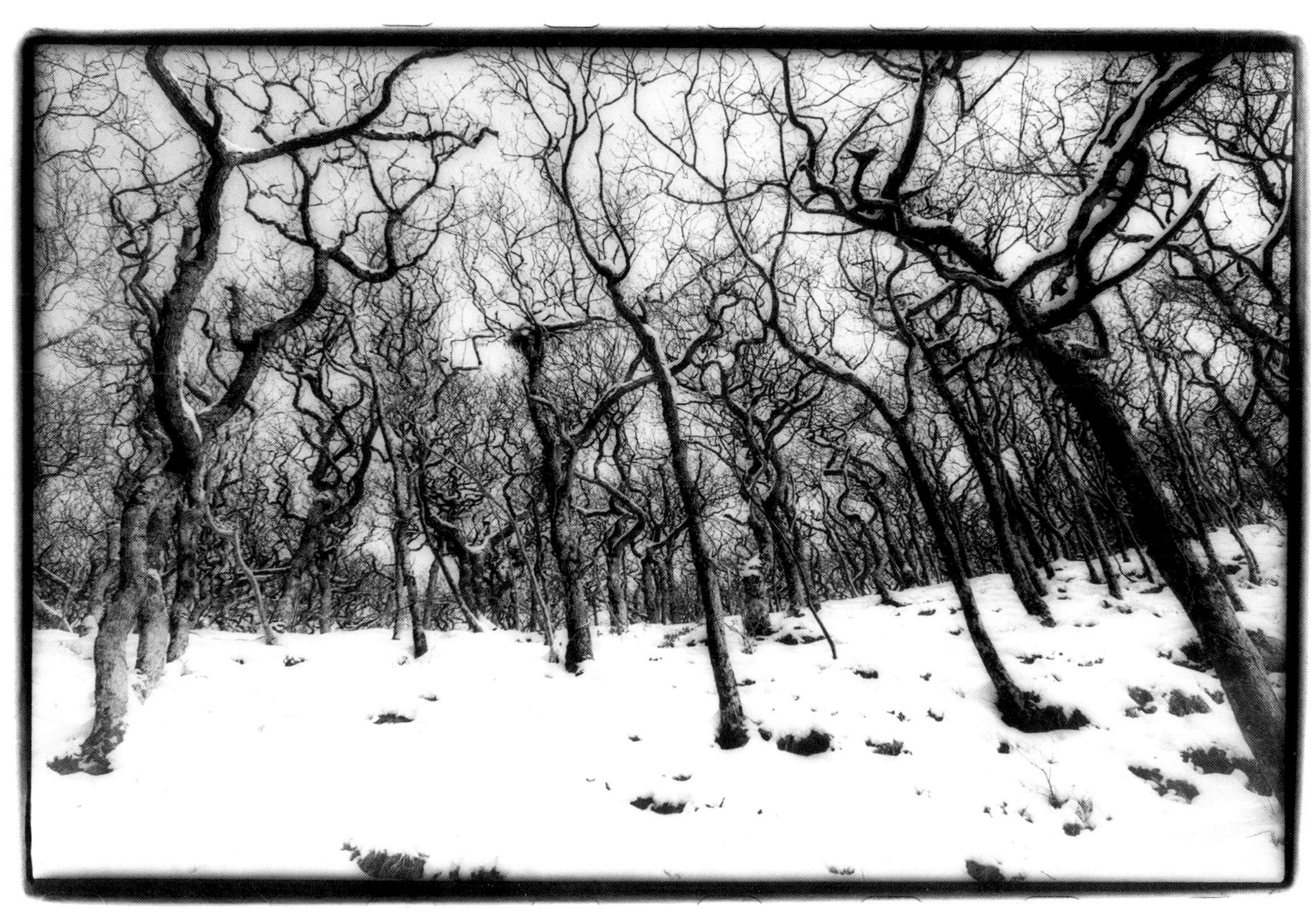

43
Scrub oak
Watersmeet, Exmoor

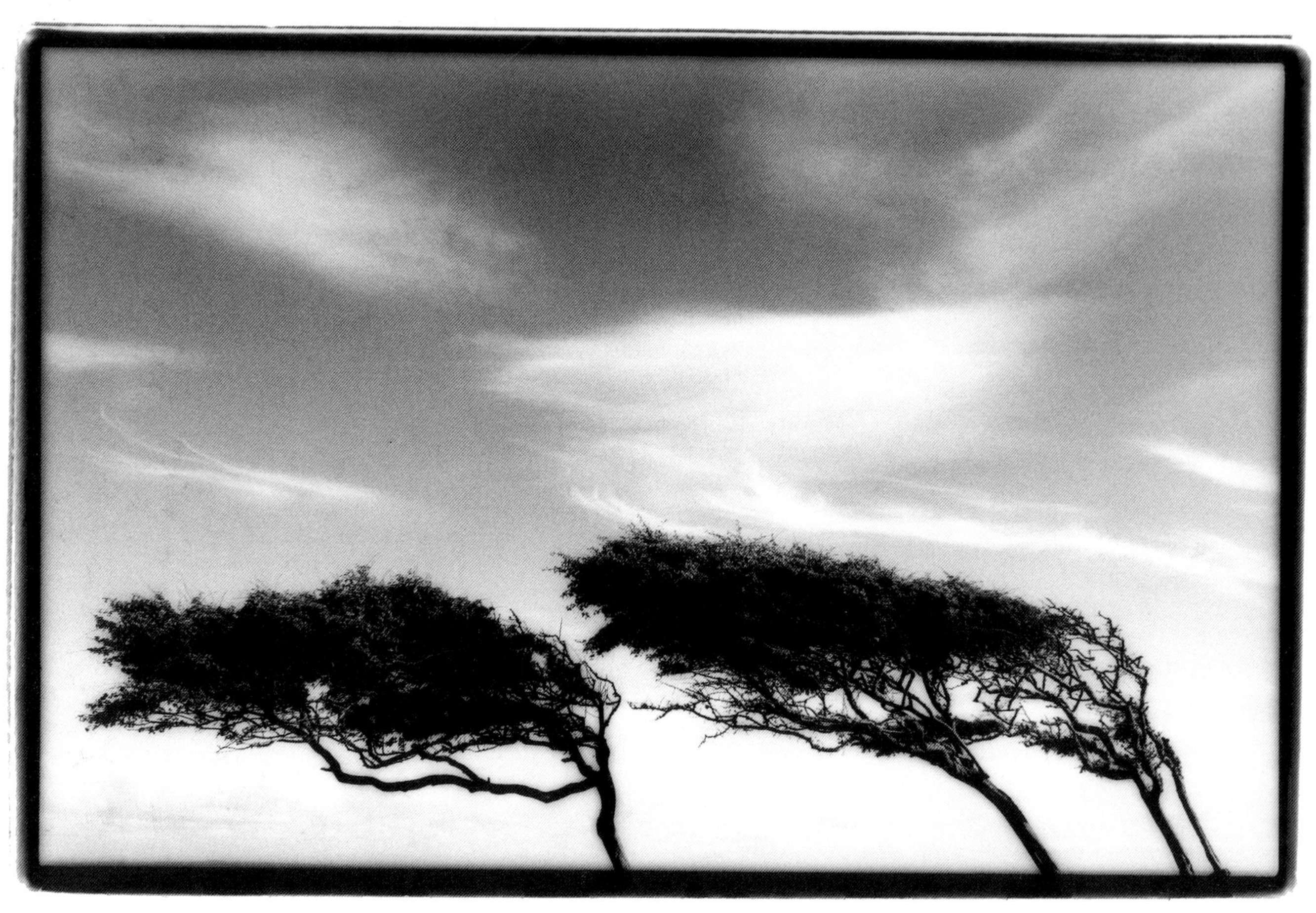

44
Windswept trees
Saunton Down

For further details of the Contemporary Portfolio series and a full catalogue of Creative Monochrome publications, please write to: Creative Monochrome Ltd, 20 St Peters Road, Croydon, Surrey, CR0 1HD, England (Tel: 0181-686 3282; Fax: 0181-681 0662; e-mail: roger@cremono.demon.co.uk)